THE
Men
OF THE
Bible

THE TOP 100

Men

OF THE

Bible

Who They Are and *What* They Mean to You Today

DREW JOSEPHS

ISBN 978-1-61626-248-8

Published by Barbour Publishing, Inc., P.O. Box 719, Uhrichsville, Ohio 44683, www.barbourbooks.com

Our mission is to publish and distribute inspirational products offering exceptional value and biblical encouragement to the masses.

Member of the
Evangelical Christian
Publishers Association

Printed in the United States of America.

To the memory of F. Scott Petersen,
a faithful expositor and teacher of God's Word,
who now walks with his Savior
among the great men of the Bible.

CONTENTS

Introduction. 11
Aaron. 13
Abel 15
Abram/Abraham 16
Adam. 19
Ahab 22
Ananias, Husband of Sapphira. 24
Andrew 25
Apollos. 27
Balaam. 28
Barnabas. 30
Bartimaeus. 32
Boaz. 33
Caiaphas 35
Caleb 37
The Centurion with a Paralyzed Servant 39
Cornelius the Centurion 40
Daniel 41
David. 44
The Demoniac of Gadara. 47
Eli 48
Elijah 49
Elisha. 52
Enoch. 55
Ezekiel 57
Ezra 59
Gideon. 61

Goliath. 63
The Good Samaritan 64
Herod. 66
Hezekiah 67
Hosea. 69
The Immoral Man of Corinth 71
Isaac. 72
Isaiah 74
Jacob 77
James, Brother of Jesus. 80
James, Son of Zebedee 81
Jeremiah. 83
Jesus. 85
Job. 88
Joel. 90
John the Apostle. 91
John the Baptist 94
Jonah 97
Jonathan. 100
Joseph of Arimathea. 102
Joseph, Foster Father of Jesus 103
Joseph, Son of Jacob. 104
Joshua 107
Josiah 110
Judas Iscariot 111
Korah. 113
Lazarus. 114
Lot. 116
Luke. 117

The Lunatic's Father. 118
Malachi 119
Manasseh 120
The Man Born Blind 121
Mark 123
Matthew. 124
Melchizedek. 125
Methuselah. 126
Micah. 127
Mordecai 129
Moses. 132
Naaman 135
Nathan. 136
Nathaniel 138
Nebuchadnezzar. 139
Nehemiah 141
Nicodemus. 143
Noah 145
Paul 148
Peter. 151
Pharaoh 154
Philemon 156
Philip the Apostle. 157
Philip the Evangelist. 158
Pontius Pilate. 159
The Prodigal Son 162
The Publican 165
The Rich Fool 166
The Rich Young Man. 167

Samson. 168
Samuel. 170
Saul, King of Israel. 172
Silas 175
Simeon. 176
Simon of Cyrene 177
Solomon. 178
Stephen 181
Thomas 182
Timothy. 183
Titus 184
Uriah 185
The Widow of Nain's Son 186
Zacchaeus. 187
Zacharias, Father of John the Baptist 188
Zechariah the Prophet 189

INTRODUCTION

Because there are many fascinating and important men in the Bible, choosing the top one hundred is somewhat subjective. Maybe this isn't the be-all-and-end-all of choices, but here are one hundred men of the Bible, most men of courage and faith, some scoundrels. Many are admirable men, flaws and all. A few were never believers or pretended to be, but their actions, leadership, or spiritual insensitivity affected many people. This collection of saints and sinners had a profound impact on Christian history and faith.

Among the one hundred, you'll find many different characters and personalities. Some you'll greet as brothers or friends, whereas others will exact a shiver of revulsion. When you read of a believing brother's trials, you may feel they speak to your own situation, or the victories found here may remind you of some of your own.

Learn from these men, be inspired by them, and avoid their mistakes. Scripture has recorded their lives to help us. May they challenge your faith and help it grow.

AARON

*Then the LORD's anger burned against Moses and he said,
"What about your brother, Aaron the Levite? I know he can
speak well. He is already on his way to meet you, and his heart
will be glad when he sees you."*

EXODUS 4:14

You could almost envy someone with a right-hand man like
Aaron: a brother who would stand by you, no matter what.
Called by God, Aaron became high priest to his younger
brother Moses' greater role of prophet, and together they led
Israel out of slavery in Egypt and toward the Promised Land.

From the time God called them, Aaron and Moses
usually appear together through the biblical story. If Moses
had been a different kind of guy, he might have sought the
limelight for himself alone, but he feared speaking out for
God. So Aaron joined him in ministry, and together they
fostered Israel's exodus.

But brotherly love has its limitations. At times, Aaron
must have deeply felt his role as second fiddle. His few
failures took place when he was not in close contact with
Moses. The first one happened following the Exodus, while
Moses lingered on Mount Sinai, receiving God's Law. The
Israelites became dissatisfied. *Where did Moses go?* they
wondered. *Maybe he has deserted us.* The crowds clamored
noisily for a new god. Perhaps Aaron feared the people, or
maybe his own doubts influenced him. But he became a
goldsmith, made a bright, shiny calf, and declared it to be
their new god.

Seeing the idolatry, God sent Moses back to confront His faithless nation. Momentarily cowed (pardon the pun), Aaron blamed the people. But he must have repented of his sin, because shortly afterward, God reconsecrated His failed priest along with His new tabernacle.

We're told of only one other time when Aaron failed—and failed hugely. He and his sister, Miriam, became angry when Moses married a Cushite woman. Jealously, they tried to increase their own importance. God responded rapidly by inflicting Miriam with leprosy. But mercifully, He did not make the high priest unclean, and Aaron got the point.

Despite Aaron's two outstanding flops, his many years of faithful service to God and Moses far outweigh his failures. If he were our employee, we might be inclined to sideline him, but God called Aaron for a purpose and did not give up. Instead, He turned the priest again to faith and used him to establish Israel's priestly line.

Have we failed? It's no time to despair. As long as we're breathing, God has a purpose for us—to glorify Him forever.

Abel brought fat portions from some of the firstborn of his flock. The LORD looked with favor on Abel and his offering, but on Cain and his offering he did not look with favor. So Cain was very angry, and his face was downcast.

GENESIS 4:4–5

You might be tempted to think, from the story of Abel and his brother, Cain, that "nice guys finish last." But if that's what you think, then you've been misled.

Abel, second son of Adam and Eve, was the family "good boy." He may have consistently done what his parents asked. Certainly he loved God deeply, for when it came time to make an offering, he brought his heavenly Father the best he had. And God smiled on him.

Cain, the elder son, may have thought, *Mom has always loved you best—and Dad does, too. Now even God is taking your side.* Quickly, brotherly competition overcame brotherly love. Feeling unloved and unaccepted because God knew that his sacrifice wasn't from the heart, Cain took out his aggression on his brother. Soon, he committed the first murder in history, and he was condemned to wander the earth for the rest of his days.

Abel didn't have a long life, but judging from the joy that accompanied his sacrifice to God, it was a successful one. Jesus commended Abel as a righteous man (see Matthew 23:35). Though Cain lived on for many more barren years after killing his brother, who will say those days and months of life were better?

If finishing last means joy in eternity, maybe being last is the first thing we should aim for.

ABRAM/ABRAHAM

The LORD had said to Abram, "Leave your country, your people and your father's household and go to the land I will show you. I will make you into a great nation and I will bless you; I will make your name great, and you will be a blessing."

GENESIS 12:1–2

Abram was a man with an immense promise: If he followed God out into the unknown, he and his descendants would be blessed. With that promise, God began to turn the childless Abram, whose name means "exalted father," into Abraham, "father of a multitude of nations."

So Abram headed for Canaan with his family. The Canaanites would have been shocked to know that God had promised their real estate to this newcomer. But Abram didn't stay long enough to put down tent pegs. He soon traveled on to Egypt to avoid a famine. There, to protect himself, Abram conveniently didn't tell Pharaoh that his lovely "sister," Sarai, was really his wife. Pharaoh brought her into his household with romantic purposes in mind. But when God confronted him with his near sin, Egypt's ruler tossed Abram out of the land.

Over time, no heir was born. So when God appeared to Abram saying, "Do not be afraid, Abram. I am your shield, your very great reward" (Genesis 15:1), Abram admitted his doubts. In polite language, he asked why he had no son. God made a covenant with Abram that he would receive both an heir (in fact, heirs too numerous to count) and a land for their possession.

But when the new covenant still didn't provide a baby, Sarai decided to help God out. As was the custom of the day, she gave Abram her servant, Hagar, as a concubine, hoping that Hagar would conceive and bear a child whom Sarai could call her own. Abram unwisely went along with the plan. But instead of improving the situation, Sarai's plan created tension within the family life and planted the seeds of enmity between the Jews (the descendants of Abraham through Isaac) and the Arab nations that would come from Hagar's son, Ishmael.

When Abram reached ninety-nine years old, God renewed His promise and changed Abram's name to Abraham and Sarai's name to Sarah, meaning "princess." As a sign of their covenant, God instituted the rite of circumcision. But despite the many good things that God gave to Abraham and Sarah, the blessing of a child still evaded them.

Abraham moved to the Negev Desert and took up residence in the territory controlled by a king named Abimelech. Again Abraham introduced his wife as his sister. And again God intervened when King Abimelech, like Pharaoh before him, took Sarah into his house. Unlike

Pharaoh, Abimelech gave Abraham money and offered him and Sarah a place to live. Eventually, Sarah bore Abraham a son, Isaac. But the camp still was not peaceful as Hagar and Sarah contended for their sons' positions. Finally, Sarah tossed Hagar and Ishmael out, and God told Abraham to allow it.

You can imagine Abraham's surprise when God commanded him to sacrifice Isaac, the son of promise. Quickly, and seemingly without argument, Abraham set out for the region of Moriah with Isaac and a bundle of wood for burning the sacrifice. Not until Abraham had laid Isaac on the altar did an angel stay his hand. God provided a ram instead, and with great relief Abraham must have removed his son from atop the wood.

When Sarah died, Abraham married again. But the children of that marriage did not change God's promise for Isaac and his descendants. Abraham arranged for Isaac's marriage to Rebekah, and then he died at the age of 175. Though scripture clearly reports Abraham's imperfections, "Abraham believed God, and it was credited to him as righteousness" (Romans 4:3). Through the patriarch's long life, we see an increasing love for God and a willingness to obey Him.

God promised much to Abraham. Some of it was a long time coming, but it came. Every promise was fulfilled. Are we willing to wait for God's blessings, growing in faith along the way? Or are we like Sarah, in such a rush that we will risk our own future? Let's walk like faithful Abraham, trusting God.

ADAM

*So the man gave names to all the livestock,
the birds of the air and all the beasts of the field.
But for Adam no suitable helper was found.*

GENESIS 2:20

Imagine being the first man ever. No one had ever done this manly thing before. One day, Adam felt God's breath in his nostrils and sort of woke up, alive for his first day. Adam lived in a God-planted garden, with animals he got to name—from springboks to hoopoes to butterflies. And God didn't even complain about any name Adam chose! But living in the Garden of Eden was still lonely. Unlike the animals, Adam didn't have a mate. So God put the first man to sleep and created a woman from his rib. *Wow* (or words to that effect), Adam must have thought. *Look what God made just for me!* He evidently recognized the connection between this new creature, this woman, and God's surgery on him, because he responded, "This is now bone of my bones and flesh of my flesh; she shall be called 'woman,' for she was taken out of man" (Genesis 2:23).

Adam and Eve lived in perfect peace with each other. Not a marital disagreement disjointed their days. They were, as you might say, joined at the rib. They were living in paradise. What could go wrong?

A lot.

Adam should have put his (bare) foot down when Eve offered him some fruit that looked suspiciously as if it had come from the one tree in the garden from which God had forbidden them. If he'd known about sin, Adam might have pointed out that God's thinking was perfect, not Eve's, and they'd better follow it. But innocent Adam knew nothing about marital discord, so he took a bite.

Suddenly, the only two humans on the planet realized they were naked. Someone (like God) might see them! So they made up clothes of fig leaves (ouch!) to cover their sin. When God came walking in the garden that evening, the couple hid from Him. For the first time, they feared their Creator. Though Adam told God he was afraid because he was naked, his sin condition, not his skin condition, was the problem.

Eve immediately came forward to blame the serpent who had tempted her to eat the fruit, so God justly cursed the snake. But Adam and Eve didn't escape punishment. Eve received pain in childbirth and a desire for her husband. He got the pain of sweating to till an earth filled with weeds. Life became drastically different from the ease and comfort they'd known in the garden.

God drove the couple out of the garden so they would not eat from the Tree of Life. An angel with a fiery sword guarded the entrance.

In their new land, the couple had two children, Cain and Abel. But like their parents, the boys sinned, and Cain became the first murderer when he became jealous of his brother and took his life. Not only did Adam and Eve lose Abel, but God also punished Cain by making him wander the earth. Eventually, he married, but Adam and Eve probably never knew their grandchildren through Cain.

Perhaps at least in part to comfort them, God gave Adam and Eve another child, Seth. Through Seth, God began the covenant line that would lead to Noah and beyond. Adam lived for 930 years, enough time to see many of these successive generations come to adulthood.

Unlike Adam, we don't have to blaze new territory. All of us have had some man we can look up to—a father, grandfather, or friend who has shown us the way. And we know the dangers of sin, perhaps because we've fallen into its trap more than once. Adam's failure in the garden left us with a sin-filled nature that entraps us all too often.

But Adam's fall was not the final word. "For as in Adam all die, even so in Christ shall all be made alive" (1 Corinthians 15:22 KJV). What we in our weakness could not do for ourselves, Jesus did at the cross. In Him, we have new life—life for eternity.

*Ahab. . .did more to provoke the LORD, the God of Israel,
to anger than did all the kings of Israel before him.*

1 KINGS 16:33

This report of scripture on Ahab's life says a lot. Because it's not as if the kings of Israel before Ahab had been a chorus of choirboys. They'd irritated God plenty. Ahab was just extraordinarily good at being bad.

Scripture doesn't detail many of Ahab's sins. But Ahab married a wicked Sidonian princess named Jezebel, who drew him and his country deeply into Baal worship. That's where the evil seems to have started.

During a drought, God commanded Elijah to appear before Ahab. Here's how the king greeted God's prophet: "Is that you, you troubler of Israel?" (1 Kings 18:17). Their relationship wasn't about to get better, for Elijah instigated a showdown between Baal and the Lord—and Jezebel's god didn't win. Elijah finished off the priests of Baal, and the drought ended along with the showdown. But by that time, both the king and queen deeply hated Elijah.

Then Ben-hadad, king of Syria, gathered thirty-two other kings and sent an imperious message to Ahab, claiming his household. Though Ahab sent back a conciliatory message, it wasn't enough for Syria's ruler: He wanted it all. But Israel's elders encouraged their weak-willed king to stand firm.

God used the wicked king to defend His people. He

promised to give Ben-hadad's huge army into Ahab's hand, then provided Israel with specific war strategies. When Israel's attack began, Ben-hadad was drunk, and the other kings did not effectively defend themselves. Syria's king barely escaped with his life.

The following spring, Ben-hadad returned. He claimed that the Israelites had won the first round because their God was a God of the hills. So God was about to show that He ruled the plains, too. Ben-hadad chose his spot, and God proved His point. In a single day, Israel killed 100,000 Syrian warriors, and the 27,000 who escaped to the city of Aphek died when the wall fell on them. But Ben-hadad was still alive, and he sued for peace. The price Syria offered seemed good to Ahab, so Ben-hadad went free. But a prophet came to Ahab and told him that his life would replace the life of Ben-hadad, whom God had desired to destroy.

When the sullen Ahab traveled to Samaria, his eyes fell on a nice vineyard that he wanted to own. But its owner, Naboth, aware that the vineyard was his patrimony, given by God, would not sell or trade. While Israel's king sulked in his room, Jezebel plotted to get the land. By paying off some men to give false testimony about the righteous Naboth, she had him killed for blasphemy.

As Israel's ruler rejoiced in his new acquisition, Elijah arrived to report that the Lord knew the truth and that dogs would lick Ahab's blood in the place where Naboth had died. The wicked king repented, for a time. But three years later, when the king of Judah enticed him into battle against Syria, Ahab listened to false prophets, who advised him to go to war. Cowardly Ahab disguised himself, but during the fight he was hit by an archer and died after hours of suffering. His body was carried to Samaria, and the blood that had gathered in his chariot was licked up by dogs, just as God had promised.

People may think that being wicked is exciting or powerful. Ahab shows us otherwise. He was a coward who was ruled by his wife. Though he won a few battles, it was not because of his own strength.

Want real strength? Serve God alone.

ANANIAS, HUSBAND OF SAPPHIRA

Now a man named Ananias, together with his wife Sapphira, also sold a piece of property. With his wife's full knowledge he kept back part of the money for himself, but brought the rest and put it at the apostles' feet.

ACTS 5:1–2

Had he been a wiser man, Ananias could have been known as generous, too. If he'd simply given whatever he and Sapphira chose and not claimed it was the full price of the property, his brethren might have praised him. But one seemingly small lie, which sought to make him seem less self-serving than he really was, turned the name Ananias into a Christian byword for greed.

When the apostle Peter confronted him with his wrongdoing against God, Ananias died. It probably wasn't just the shock of being found out—his was a godly judgment that kept other early Christians honest. When Sapphira died in the same manner, the people had no doubts about God's opinion of the couple's deeds.

Unlike Ananias and his wife, we may not die when we do wrong. But our deceptions hurt us nevertheless. God may not respond as quickly as He did with Ananias, but He does not ignore our sin. Will it take a lightning bolt from heaven to command our obedience, or just a word to our hearts from our Savior?

ANDREW

The first thing Andrew did was to find his brother Simon and tell him, "We have found the Messiah" (that is, the Christ).

JOHN 1:41

How eager are you to tell others about Jesus? Instead of delighting in the prospect of such work, many of us struggle with what could be called "analysis paralysis." We worry about the best way to do it and never broadcast the message that Andrew spoke so simply.

Perhaps Andrew had a God-given predisposition to seek the Lord, but he had something even more important: a God-given mentor. The apostle John tells us that Andrew was a disciple of John the Baptist. For how long? Evidently it was long enough for the prophet to make quite an impression on this young man of Galilee.

We can only imagine what Andrew learned from John the Baptist. Perhaps he was among those who heard John take the Pharisees to task, saying, "[You] brood of vipers!" (Matthew 3:7 NKJV). We can be sure that Andrew heard the prophet's heralding of the coming Messiah. It was in the very forefront of all that John taught—and he declared it *emphatically*! He may have had a Greek name, but Andrew was more than Jewish enough to know about the Messiah. No doubt he knew about Him well before he met John.

Then came a day when Andrew heard his mentor say, "Behold the Lamb of God!" Scripture says, "The two disciples heard him speak, and they followed Jesus. Then Jesus turned, and seeing them following, said to them, 'What do you seek?' They said to Him, 'Rabbi' (which is to say, when translated, Teacher), 'where are You staying?' He said to them, 'Come and see.' They came and saw where He was staying, and remained with Him that day" (John 1:37–39 NKJV).

What was this first meeting like, and what did Jesus say? Whatever happened, it had a profound impact on Andrew, because not long after, he declared to his brother Simon, "We have found the Messiah." Andrew had discovered his true Mentor—and much more than that! Convinced of who Jesus was, Andrew brought his own brother to meet Him. Though Jesus Himself could have easily arranged the meeting, He allowed Andrew the privilege of introducing his elder brother to the Messiah.

Like Andrew, all of us bring others face-to-face with Jesus, but only in direct proportion to our conviction that we have found our own personal Lord and Savior. Is our conviction as firm as Andrew's?

APOLLOS

Meanwhile a Jew named Apollos, a native of Alexandria, came to Ephesus. He was a learned man, with a thorough knowledge of the Scriptures.

ACTS 18:24

Though Apollos knew the Old Testament scriptures well, something was missing. He'd been taught about Jesus but only knew the baptism of John. This eloquent man had yet to be acquainted with the workings of the Holy Spirit. So two leaders of the Ephesian church, a couple named Priscilla and Aquila, brought Apollos up to date on the work God was doing and the impact the Spirit had on Christians.

The golden-tongued preacher must have listened carefully and obeyed God's will, for when he moved on to Achaia, the Ephesian church leaders wrote a note of introduction to the believers there. We know that Apollos's improved ministry was influential in the Corinthian church, because some of its quarrelsome members claimed to follow him instead of Paul.

Like Apollos, are we able to admit that we don't have all the truth grasped in our hands? When another Christian points out a flaw in our thinking, can we humbly listen, compare that correction to scripture, and perhaps change course? Being able to do so may enable us to touch more lives for Jesus.

BALAAM

When the donkey saw the angel of the LORD, she lay down under Balaam, and he was angry and beat her with his staff.

NUMBERS 22:27

Imagine being a prophet who's dumber than a donkey. That's Balaam's reputation in scripture. And it was well earned by a man who wasn't quite faithful to God.

Following the Exodus, as the Israelites entered Moab, fearful King Balak hired Balaam, a Midianite prophet, to curse the invading nation. God ordered the prophet to go to the king but only speak His words, for He knew that Balaam was less than wholeheartedly faithful.

As Balaam headed toward Moab, God became angry (perhaps because the prophet was already thinking of ways to evade His command) and sent an angel to block his path. Balaam couldn't see the angel, but his donkey could. Three times, Balaam's donkey tried to avoid the heavenly being. Each time, the prophet struck the beast. Then God allowed them to have a conversation, and the donkey pointed out the angel. When Balaam saw it, he recognized his sin and offered to return home. Again he was warned to report God's truth.

Three times, Balak had the prophet offer sacrifices, hoping to get him to curse Israel, but each time Balaam obeyed God and blessed the nation. But on the sly, the false prophet suggested that Moab lead the Israelites astray by encouraging them to worship Baal (see Numbers 31:16). His plan worked. So when Israel attacked Moab's allies, the Midianites, Balaam was put to the sword.

Balaam was partly faithful to God. But when it served his own purposes, disobedience was still an option. Are we, like him, only willing to listen to the commands we like to hear, or do we follow God completely?

BARNABAS

*Joseph, a Levite from Cyprus, whom the apostles
called Barnabas (which means Son of Encouragement),
sold a field he owned and brought the money
and put it at the apostles' feet.*

ACTS 4:36–37

From the moment he appears in scripture, it's obvious that
Barnabas is an admirable man. Scripture describes him as "a
good man, full of the Holy Spirit and faith" (Acts 11:24).
First-century Christians didn't call this church leader "Son
of Encouragement" for nothing; look at his ministry, and
you'll understand how he got his nickname.

Saul, the former persecutor of the church who became
known as Paul, benefited from Barnabas's warmheartedness.
When everyone else in the church worried about whether
Saul's conversion was genuine, Barnabas collected the
new convert and brought him to the apostles. The Son of
Encouragement must also have been a risk taker for his Lord,
because if he had been wrong about Saul, Barnabas would
have been bringing enemy number one into the church.

Next, the church leaders in Jerusalem sent Barnabas
to Antioch to check out some fellow Cypriots who were
preaching to the Greeks (unlike other Christian preachers
at the time who were preaching only to the Jews).
Barnabas approved of what he found in Antioch, as many
Greeks were being converted, and he later brought Paul
to Antioch. For a year the two taught the new converts,

leaving only briefly to take a relief collection to Jerusalem. After they returned, God sent them out on their first missionary journey, to Galatia.

During this adventurous journey, they were driven out of Antioch of Pisidia, fled from Iconium, healed a man at Lystra, and were declared gods there. But Paul was stoned in Lystra, so they kept moving, returning eventually to Antioch. There they confronted Judaizers, who demanded that the Christian community be circumcised.

Sent on, they traveled to Jerusalem to report on their mission. There they again faced Judaizers and, with Peter's support, convinced the church leaders not to require Gentile circumcision.

Finally, Paul and Barnabas went their separate ways after a disagreement about having John Mark as a companion on their missions. John Mark had left the first missionary journey midstream, and Barnabas evidently forgave him, but Paul was not ready to have him back. So Barnabas and John Mark went to Cyprus together—and Barnabas's faith in his young companion was fulfilled, because John Mark went on to become the writer of the Gospel of Mark.

Barnabas was exactly what the early church needed—a wise, patient leader. Wouldn't we like a handful of them in each of our own churches? Even more, wouldn't we like to be one of them? From Barnabas, we learn what it means to encourage others in faith and leadership. Like him, do we trust in God's plan, no matter what we face? Do we put faith in His working it out through the imperfect people we deal with daily?

BARTIMAEUS

Then they came to Jericho. As Jesus and his disciples, together
with a large crowd, were leaving the city, a blind man,
Bartimaeus (that is, the Son of Timaeus), was sitting by the
roadside begging. When he heard that it was Jesus of Nazareth,
he began to shout, "Jesus, Son of David, have mercy on me!"

MARK 10:46–47

As Jesus and His disciples left Jericho, a large crowd
surrounded them. Someone whispered in the ear of a blind
beggar sitting on the side of the road that Jesus was passing
by. Destitute Bartimaeus probably wasn't anyone's image
of an ideal disciple, but from his cry to the Savior, "Son of
David" (a messianic title), we know that he knew who Jesus
was and wanted Him for his Master.

Despite being discouraged by Jesus' followers,
Bartimaeus persisted, crying out even more loudly.
Amazingly, Jesus called the beggar to Himself. Bartimaeus
jumped up, dashed to the Savior, and begged for his sight.
Jesus swiftly healed him, commending him for his faith,
and the man rushed to follow his Lord.

Are we persistent, or can others turn us aside from
crying out to the Master for our needs? If what we seek
is God's will, we can follow the beggar's example and
unrelentingly call on Jesus. Will He fail to answer us?

So [Ruth] went out and began to glean in the fields behind the harvesters. As it turned out, she found herself working in a field belonging to Boaz, who was from the clan of Elimelech.

RUTH 2:3

The young Moabite woman named Ruth must have been the talk of the town when she came to Bethlehem with her mother-in-law, Naomi. Boaz must have heard of the foreign woman's care for her in-law even before Ruth began gleaning his field. Then one of his men told him of Ruth's modest and unassuming behavior. So this kindhearted man watched out for her, telling her to stay near his women for protection and to drink from the vessels his men filled with water. He even ordered his men to give her extra grain.

Confronted about his concern for her, he replied to Ruth, "May the LORD repay you for what you have done. May you be richly rewarded by the LORD, the God of Israel, under whose wings you have come to take refuge" (Ruth 2:12). Perhaps Boaz was unaware that he himself would be part of the reward.

At home that evening, Naomi informed Ruth that Boaz was one of their kinsman-redeemers—a close relative of her husband, Elimelech—who could come to the widow's aid by marrying her. But instead of desiring Boaz for herself, Naomi put her daughter-in-law in Boaz's path, sending her to the threshing floor to essentially make a marriage proposal to the kinsman-redeemer by sleeping at his feet.

In the morning, Boaz met with the closest kinsman-redeemer in the family. When the man turned down the opportunity to act on his claim, Boaz bought Elimelech's land and promised to marry Ruth.

For his faithfulness, Boaz gained not only a wonderful young wife, but also a place in history, for he became the great-grandfather of King David and has a place in the lineage of the Messiah.

Boaz took a risk, marrying a foreigner who might not have remained faithful to the Lord. But he listened with his heart and spirit and willingly paid a price to bring her into his home. How willing are we to risk ourselves to do God's will when He calls us to do so? How kind are our hearts when we encounter others in need?

CAIAPHAS

During the high priesthood of Annas and Caiaphas,
the word of God came to John son of Zechariah in the desert.

LUKE 3:2

Chronologically, this is the first mention of the ungodly
high priest who held authority during Jesus' ministry.
Caiaphas had gotten the position when the Romans
deposed his father-in-law, Annas. Because some Jews still
viewed Annas as the high priest, maybe Caiaphas always
felt as if Annas were looking over his shoulder. Certainly
the Romans were: They wanted to keep a tight lid on the
rebellious Jews, or they'd all lose their jobs.

Maybe that explains why Caiaphas acted more like a
political leader than a religious one. He worried more about
what people thought than about what was right. So when
Jesus came along, it wasn't hard for him to make some
really bad decisions.

When Jesus raised Lazarus from the dead, Israel's
religious leaders, the Sanhedrin, got really concerned. This
might lead to rebellion. The Romans would blame it all on
them and replace them with leaders who could keep the
peace. They envisioned themselves losing power, as Annas
had.

Caiaphas offered a solution—kill Jesus. There was
only one problem: Under Roman law, the Jews couldn't
kill anyone. So these selfish leaders held a kangaroo court
in which Caiaphas accepted any testimony that would

rid them of the Galilean. Then he passed Jesus on to the Roman authorities, who were also concerned about keeping the Jews quiet and thus found it expedient for Jesus to die.

After Jesus' death, His apostles still pestered the high priest by preaching the good news. Twice, Caiaphas arrested some of the apostles but found himself unable to do more than warn them not to preach. We hear no more of him in scripture after the early chapters of the book of Acts.

Caiaphas was a church leader gone wrong. His faith never informed his actions, so it's hard to believe he was anything but an unbeliever. Would we have people say that of us, or will we commit to acting out our faith in love and trust in God?

[Caleb said,] "But I wholly followed the Lord my God."

Imagine having to wait forty years for the realization of your dream. That's how long it took for Caleb, Joshua's comrade-in-arms, to obtain Mount Hebron in the land of Canaan. Quite likely, Caleb first discovered his heart's desire while spying out the land of Canaan with Joshua and the ten others whom Moses dispatched for that purpose. He was then forty-five years old.

Caleb and Joshua's fellow spies issued a disheartening report about the land, and Israel tragically succumbed to their fear, to their own disgrace and demise. Caleb proclaimed that he (and Joshua) had followed the Lord wholeheartedly. Together the two faithful men delivered a favorable, determined report that almost led to their being stoned, were it not for the intervention of God Himself (see Numbers 14). So began a miserable wandering in the desert for forty long years; one year for each day the spies were in the land of Canaan. Everyone Joshua and Caleb knew fell in that desert wasteland.

Then came the day when Canaan was finally apportioned among the twelve tribes of Israel. While Judah was receiving its portion, Caleb boldly stepped forward and told Joshua, "You know the word which the Lord said to Moses the man of God concerning you and me in Kadesh Barnea. . . . Now therefore, give me this mountain" (Joshua

14:6, 12 NKJV). Caleb hadn't given up on his dream, and he was prepared to fight for it if he had to. He said, "And now, here I am this day, eighty-five years old. As yet I am as strong this day as on the day that Moses sent me; just as my strength was then, so now is my strength for war, both for going out and for coming in" (Joshua 14:10–11 NKJV).

There was no hesitation on Joshua's part. Evidently, Caleb had shared his desire to possess Mount Hebron with Moses, and Moses had agreed. Joshua obviously knew about this and gladly gave Mount Hebron to his dear friend.

It has been said that while Caleb's feet were treading the desert, his heart was atop the heights of Mount Hebron. God has a dream in mind for each of us, just as He did for Caleb. It might not require us to wait forty years for its fulfillment; it does require that we follow the Lord our God wholeheartedly and commit to our part as He enables us and leads us to the realization of our dreams.

THE CENTURION WITH A PARALYZED SERVANT

The centurion sent friends to [Jesus], saying to Him, "Lord, do not trouble Yourself, for I am not worthy that You should enter under my roof. Therefore I did not even think myself worthy to come to You. But say the word, and my servant will be healed."

LUKE 7:6–7 NKJV

Although he was not Jewish, the centurion loved the Jewish people and even built them a synagogue. The Jewish elders begged Jesus earnestly to come and heal the Gentile's servant, who was dear to him and gravely ill. Such regard for a Roman centurion was extraordinary!

Jesus proceeded at once with them. He wasn't far from the centurion's home when he met some friends of the centurion, who passed along this message: "Lord, do not trouble Yourself, for I am not worthy that You should enter under my roof. Therefore I did not even think myself worthy to come to You. But say the word, and my servant will be healed. For I also am a man placed under authority, having soldiers under me. And I say to one, 'Go,' and he goes; and to another, 'Come,' and he comes; and to my servant, 'Do this,' and he does it" (Luke 7:6–8 NKJV).

Most folks wanted Jesus to prove Himself. Not this man. He simply said, "Just say the word." He knew enough about Jesus to believe that if Jesus spoke words of healing, even from afar, it would be done. Perhaps this is why Jesus said, "I say to you, I have not found such great faith, not even in Israel!" (Luke 7:9 NKJV).

It has been said that the greatest challenge any Christian faces is to believe in the trustworthiness of God's Word. How much do we trust?

CORNELIUS THE CENTURION

The angel answered [Cornelius], "Your prayers and gifts to the poor have come up as a memorial offering before God."

ACTS 10:4

Gentile! The word isn't usually used as a compliment. In the time of Jesus, Jews weren't to associate with Gentiles. During the very earliest days, the church consisted of Jews only, beginning as a sect of Judaism.

Converts to Judaism were obviously Gentiles. Scripture tells us that Cornelius was one of these, although his conversion might not have encompassed all the rituals. Male Gentiles who did not undergo circumcision were referred to as "God fearers."

Even so, Cornelius exhibited genuine faith in the God of Abraham, Isaac, and Jacob, and a fervor for prayer and almsgiving. In time, a heavenly messenger appeared to him and told him that his prayers and alms had come up for a memorial before God. He was instructed to send for the apostle Peter. Meanwhile, God gave Peter a vision in which he was told not to call anything unclean that God had made clean. This opened the way for Peter to visit Cornelius and baptize him and his entire household—the first Gentile converts to Christianity!

Could it be that God chose a military commander as the first Gentile convert to Christianity because the man was accustomed to giving respect? For all his authority, note the respect Cornelius showed Peter. How well do we follow Cornelius's example toward godly messengers in our day?

DANIEL

Then Daniel answered, and said before the king,
"Let your gifts be for yourself, and give your rewards
to another; yet I will read the writing to the king,
and make known to him the interpretation."

DANIEL 5:17 NKJV

The event in this verse didn't happen during the first part of Daniel's life. His character-defining moment came when he was a thoroughly experienced man who had completed decades of service as prime minister to the king of Babylon. But in a life marked by devotion to duty, above all, the prophet showed his devotion to the God of his native Israel.

Daniel's worldly success began in a way that he probably never would have dreamed. As part of the fortunes of conquest, Daniel found himself taken captive and forced to march to the distant heathen land of Babylon. No doubt this was a wrenching experience for the devout young man. Suddenly, he found himself immersed in a culture foreign to all that he knew, a culture steeped in paganism. If that weren't enough, Daniel was chosen to serve the king of Babylon, to be taught the language and writings of the Chaldeans, and to take a Babylonian name (Daniel 1:3–7). Can we possibly appreciate how utterly repulsive all this was to Daniel? Yet he had no choice, nor did his companions, Hanniah, Azariah, and Mishael. Escape was impossible, and the penalty for any such attempt would have been severe. Eventually, Daniel developed an allegiance to King Nebuchadnezzar. What this king spoke was law without question.

Despite his situation, through God's enabling, Daniel managed to develop an agreeable disposition without compromising his obedience to the Lord. He built a reputation of the highest integrity, discharging his duties diligently and honestly.

God also blessed Daniel with a particular ability to see beyond immediate reality and interpret dreams. At least twice, Daniel interpreted dreams for Nebuchadnezzar. On one of these occasions, Daniel saved not only the lives of the wise men of Chaldea, but his own life, too (see Daniel 2). Apparently, the keen wisdom God gave the prophet made him the most respected and influential of all the wise men in Babylon. Yet Daniel never let his ability go to his head. The more deference he showed, the higher his stature rose in the kingdom. Daniel's life was undergirded by faithful prayer and meditation upon the Law God gave to Moses.

Then came the scene in the great banquet hall of King Belshazzar. The handwriting is on the wall. The king's knees are knocking. What does it mean? Who will interpret it? The queen knows exactly whom to call. "O king, live forever! Do not let your thoughts trouble you, nor let your countenance change. There is a man in your kingdom in whom is the Spirit of the Holy God. And in the days of your father, light and understanding and wisdom, like the wisdom of the gods, were found in him; and King Nebuchadnezzar your father—your father the king—made him chief of the magicians, astrologers, Chaldeans, and soothsayers. Inasmuch as an excellent spirit, knowledge, understanding, interpreting dreams, solving riddles, and explaining enigmas were found in this Daniel, whom the king named Belteshazzar, now let Daniel be called, and he will give the interpretation" (Daniel 5:10–12 NKJV).

Daniel's whole character seems to converge in this moment. The summation of all that he is as a man shows through in the few words he speaks to Belshazzar. The king has promised gifts and the highest recognition to anyone who can answer the riddle. Daniel is not after a reward but boldly makes clear the revelation of God, whom the king has defied by his desecration of sacred vessels from the temple in Jerusalem. Not only is Daniel correct in his interpretation but he is fearless in exposing the king's wickedness and his fate. The rewards of the king pale in comparison to God's rewards.

Although he never returned to Judah or Jerusalem, this man of God shone as a great light in pagan Babylon.

Not many of us will rise to the stature of a Daniel, but he himself would tell us that unswerving devotion to God and not worldly fame is what counts most in our walk with the Creator.

DAVID

He raised up unto them David to be their king;
to whom also he gave testimony, and said,
I have found David the son of Jesse, a man after
mine own heart, which shall fulfil all my will.

ACTS 13:22 KJV

Even before David came to power as king of Israel, he had God's full confidence. David started out well. The former shepherd boy began by serving King Saul and fought Goliath, bringing honor to God and destruction to the Philistines. Saul made David a military commander, hoping he would be killed, but the people loved the new commander's battlefield success.

Jealous Saul tried to kill David, so the young warrior fled and ended up hiding in a cave. But not alone. His family and many whom Saul had treated badly joined him—about four hundred men. As civil war began, Saul must have realized he had trained his own enemy! Yet throughout the battles, David never harmed God's anointed king.

Finally, fearing for his life, David became a mercenary for Philistia but avoided fighting Israel. Instead, he made certain that no one lived to tell the Philistine king, Achish, that David was battling the other peoples of the land when he was supposed to be attacking Israel.

While David retrieved two of his wives, who had been kidnapped by the Amalekites, the Philistines fought the Israelites. Badly wounded, Saul killed himself, and three of his sons died in combat.

David was anointed king over Judah, but Ish-bosheth, Saul's only surviving son, became king of Israel. When two of his own men killed Ish-bosheth, David received Israel's crown.

In Jerusalem, David's faithful walk became much less consistent. The new king, who already had three wives, built a beautiful home, took many more wives and concubines, and went out to battle and defeated the Philistines. Then David brought the ark of the covenant to his capital city, in hopes that it would bring blessing.

But while his army defeated the Ammonites and Syrians, David remained in Jerusalem, where he was attracted by a beautiful married woman, Bathsheba. He fell quickly into sin with her, and when she discovered she was pregnant, David plotted to have her husband, Uriah, die. His plot was successful, and he quickly married the widow.

Greatly displeased, God rebuked David through the voice of the prophet Nathan. The prophet reminded David of God's care for him throughout his life and declared that because of his sin, David's house would not have peace.

Nathan's prophecy was fulfilled among David's children, as God had promised. His illegitimate child by Bathsheba died. His daughter Tamar was raped by her half brother, Amnon. Tamar's full brother, Absalom, then murdered Amnon and started a conspiracy to take the throne from his father, who had to flee from Jerusalem. Only when Absalom was killed could his grieving father return to his throne.

Again David sinned, taking a census of his people. Perhaps having learned from his tryst with Bathsheba, he immediately confessed to God. God gave him three choices of punishment. The humbled king decided to receive his punishment from the hand of God, so David had to fight a pestilence rather than another nation. Mercifully, God did not send David the third choice: three years of famine. When David built an altar to God to avert the plague, God ended it.

As David's life dwindled, his son Adonijah attempted to grab the throne, which was intended for Solomon. Only the intervention of Nathan and Bathsheba saved Solomon's inheritance. David ended the issue by declaring Solomon his heir and having him anointed as king.

When we read of David's life, we begin to understand that our lives are not made up of compartments. We cannot keep our work life in one box and family life in another. When David sinned in his personal life, it affected his rule. When he was faithful, everyone benefited. Our lives need that consistency that glorifies God.

Though David had some major life failures, God made

him one of the most powerful kings in Israel and brought the Messiah from his line. Though any man fails, God does not desert him—that is true for us as it was for David.

THE DEMONIAC OF GADARA

*Then they came to Jesus, and saw the one
who had been demon-possessed and had the legion,
sitting and clothed and in his right mind.*

MARK 5:15 NKJV

Is there a more desperate biblical figure than the out-of-control, demon-possessed man of Gadara? Infiltrated by a horde of demons, who called themselves "Legion" (Mark 5:9), he had been reduced to a humiliating state and separated from home and friends. It's likely that this unhappy fellow had toyed with sin until it had a stranglehold on him.

It has been said that whenever Jesus confronted demons, they did what even the religious leaders of the day refused to do: They acknowledged Him to be the Son of God. It was no different in this case.

From the start, Jesus was in control of the entire situation, demons and all. Imagine the freedom the man felt when the demons left him! Once the man's sanity was restored, Jesus and the apostles clothed him. He begged to go with Jesus, but the Master sent him home to share the message of his healing (see Mark 5:19).

This man keenly knew what he had been saved from. If Jesus has saved us, do we comprehend what we have been saved from, and does it drive us to share our faith with others?

ELI

Year after year this man went up from his town to worship and sacrifice to the LORD Almighty at Shiloh, where Hophni and Phinehas, the two sons of Eli, were priests of the LORD.

1 SAMUEL 1:3

The household of a less-than-faithful priest, whose sons scripture describes as "worthless men" (1 Samuel 2:12 ESV), seems an unlikely place for the budding prophet Samuel to grow up.

Eli wouldn't have gotten the Father of the Year award. His sons bullied worshippers to do wrong, and they became involved with religious prostitutes. Their father must have received many complaints. When he finally took his sons to task, clearly it was too little, too late. God blamed Eli, who had failed to stop the boys' sin when they were young. God promised that the two sons would die young and on the same day.

But God not only raised up a new priest to take Hophni's and Phinehas's places, He graciously let Eli rear his replacement—Samuel, who was faithful to God.

This gentle, caring man had put his sons' wills before the Father's, with disastrous results. Will we learn from him? Or will we nurture our children but fail to correct them? If so, like Eli, we may find them overwhelming our households with sin. Are we raising "worthless men" or children who will glorify God?

ELIJAH

So [Elijah] said, "I have been very zealous for the LORD God of hosts; for the children of Israel have forsaken Your covenant, torn down Your altars, and killed Your prophets with the sword. I alone am left; and they seek to take my life."

1 KINGS 19:10 NKJV

Of all God's prophets, none is more striking than Elijah, the prophet of fire! Like all the other prophets, he appeared at a critical juncture in biblical history. The prophets' chief function was to challenge the people of Judah and Israel to repent of their sins and return to the Lord after they had plunged headlong into apostasy. Often, prophets were directed by God to challenge the people in dramatic ways, such as Isaiah's walking naked in public (see Isaiah 20) or Jeremiah's smashing a clay pot (see Jeremiah 19). These spectacles were definitely attention getters, and they were effective to a certain extent.

In scripture, Elijah seemingly appears from out of nowhere, as was frequently the case with prophets. God sent him to testify against the northern kingdom of Israel and its evil king, Ahab. From the time of Jeroboam, Israel's first king, the northern kingdom had been on a continual descent into iniquity. Ahab and his malevolent wife, Jezebel, represented the very worst in all Israel. Elijah was sent by God to apply the "dive brakes" and lead the kingdom out of its downward plunge toward hell.

Prophets were not "nice guys," nor were they intended to be. They were deadly serious in their preaching and gave no quarter to those who opposed their message, which was literally a matter of life and death. This was certainly so with Elijah. Consider his courage and boldness as he confronted an entire nation and their king, thinking himself the only one left capable of taking a stand. Such strength would not have been possible or properly applied were it not for God's enabling and leading.

In his very first prophecy, Elijah stated emphatically to Ahab, "As the LORD God of Israel lives, before whom I stand, there shall not be dew nor rain these years, except at my word" (1 Kings 17:1 NKJV). The words "before whom I stand" can also be interpreted as "in whose presence I stand." Elijah had intimacy with God, an intimacy that came by diligently seeking the God of Abraham, Isaac, and Jacob. Evidently, the more Elijah focused on seeking God, the closer he was drawn to Him and the more zealous he grew toward Him.

This is what Elijah carried with him to the heights of

Mount Carmel. This drove him to display matchless faith in contrast to the heathen priests of Baal. "You had better work a little harder, boys," he railed against them. "Perhaps your god has gone on a trip and can't hear you." Not the words of a tepid, halfhearted soul. The victory wrought by God that day atop Mount Carmel was a triumph of His power at work through the witness of the one man He steeled for the task.

But Elijah was no superhero. It's comforting to know that he was a man "with a nature like ours" (James 5:17 NKJV) and not some superhuman. Still, God caused an outpouring of miracles to occur through Elijah as He did through Moses. When the time of his departure from this world came, Elijah was carried alive into heaven in a chariot of fire. The prophet Malachi tells us that Elijah will return "before the coming of the great and dreadful day of the LORD" (Malachi 4:5 NKJV). Is it any wonder that he alone accompanied Moses at the meeting with Jesus on the Mount of Transfiguration (see Matthew 17:1–13)?

None of us may be called to stand as boldly as Elijah did; nor are we likely to be swept up in a chariot of fire. Nevertheless, each of us has been given what Augustine called a "God-sized hole" in our hearts. If we pursue God as the primary objective of our lives, God will fill that void with His holy presence. Then He will enable us to zealously follow in the footsteps of Elijah by fitting us for the works He has prepared for us beforehand to accomplish (see Ephesians 2:10).

ELISHA

*Elisha said, "Please let a double
portion of your spirit be upon me."*

2 Kings 2:9 NKJV

What a moment in biblical history! Both Elijah and Elisha
are about to be engulfed in a spectacular supernatural
event: Elijah's departure from this planet. Elijah, caring
to the very last, asks his disciple if there is anything he
can do for him before he departs. As if he's always known
what to ask for, Elisha asks his master for a double portion
of his spirit. "You have asked a hard thing," says Elijah.
"Nevertheless, if you see me when I am taken from you, it
shall be so for you" (2 Kings 2:10 NKJV).

Suddenly, a chariot of fire and horses of fire appeared
and carried Elijah away, body and soul, into heaven. What
an incredible event this must have been. Yet it was over as
quickly as it happened. Elijah's mantle now lay at Elisha's
feet. Elijah had cast this same garment over Elisha when
he first came upon him as he was plowing his father's field.
The prophet of fire had passed the torch to his successor.

Elisha, dazed by what he'd just witnessed, stooped
down and picked up the mantle. He took it not as some
relic to be worshipped, but rather as an emblem of the
legacy Elijah had left him and the solemn responsibility he
had conferred upon him. Elisha hadn't asked for wealth or
prestige. He'd asked to be amply fitted for service to God.
Taking up Elijah's mantle, he carried on his master's work,

serving as a father to his fellow prophets and confronting the same enemies Elijah had. His work was twice as long as Elijah's, with twice as many miracles, and so much more would be required of him. Can there be any doubt that the Holy Spirit led Elisha to ask for what he did?

Elisha returned to the Jordan and struck it with Elijah's mantle. He simultaneously invoked the God of Elijah by saying, "Where is the LORD God of Elijah?" (2 Kings 2:14 NKJV). The waters parted, and Elisha walked across to the other side. When his fellow prophets saw him, they knew the spirit of Elijah rested on Elisha (2 Kings 2:15 NKJV). It's interesting that the first miracle Elisha performed was the very last performed by his master.

In the Bible, miracles came intermittently, in clusters, most notably during the ministries of Moses, Elijah, Elisha, and Jesus. The power to perform miracles was conferred by God to authenticate the call He had given each one of them. Miracles also demonstrated a mighty movement of God's hand at these junctures in biblical history.

Elisha dealt with the rebellious house of Jeroboam and the northern kingdom of Israel. Thus, some of the miracles he performed were meant to confront and punish, as in the case of the scoffing youths recorded in 2 Kings 2:23–25. What at first seems like an overreaction is, upon further investigation, justified. The youths lived in Bethel, the site of one of the two calf idols Jeroboam had made. It's said the locals didn't like being rebuked for the idol's presence, so the youths were simply acting out on their parents' disdain for Elisha and God; hence, the dramatic bear attack.

In most of the miracles he performed, Elisha demonstrated God's concern for ordinary people and the nation. A stunning example of this would be the story of the Syrian force that came to capture Elisha in Dothan (see 2 Kings 6:8–23). Here we see God's mercy in reassuring Elisha's servant, but also in sparing the Syrians whom He had blinded. Elisha led them right to the king of Israel but protected them from his wrath. Elisha understood that God's intent is to draw others to Himself either by His discipline or by His mercy.

Elisha had learned well from his master and predecessor and thus carried high and nobly the torch passed to him. His example could be summed up in the words of John L. Mason, who counseled that we're to follow no man (or woman) any closer than that person follows Jesus.

ENOCH

*After he begot Methuselah, Enoch walked with God
three hundred years, and had sons and daughters.*

GENESIS 5:22 NKJV

What does it mean to walk with God? We have no better
example than the biblical figure of Enoch. Though little
is written about Enoch in scripture, much can be inferred
about his life and character.

In a day when we're told that character isn't all that
important, let's remember that by our character we make
visible the kingdom of God. For those of us who claim the
title *Christian*, making God's kingdom visible is our life's
purpose.

Enoch also lived at a time when character wasn't
valued very much. In fact, humanity was on a slippery
slope toward hell. Cain's descendants were becoming
more and more corrupt. Their ungodliness caused a
gross degeneration of the human race. Before long, their
corruption had even begun to contaminate the godly
descendants of Seth, Adam and Eve's third child. Eventually,
God could no longer bear such widespread iniquity and
passed judgment in the form of a great flood. Enoch's great-
grandson Noah and his family were the only ones who
escaped that awful event.

Scripture tells us that after Enoch fathered his son
Methuselah, he walked with God. Presumably, up until
Methuselah's birth, Enoch lived no differently than other

men of his time. He might not have been so vile as others, but he only walked *after* God instead of walking *with* Him. Bible commentator Matthew Henry writes that walking with God is "to make God's Word our rule and His glory our end in all our actions." Scripture doesn't tell us what caused this change in Enoch's walk, but it was probably something extraordinary. Perhaps the repulsiveness of humanity's increasing degeneration drove him nearer to God. Sanctification is a series of steps from grace to grace.

The epistle of Jude tells us that Enoch prophesied against those of his generation and predicted a dire outcome for them. Undoubtedly, this cast him in a bad light with the world of his time. Without trying to be self-righteous, Enoch may have become as repugnant to the world as it had become to him. His profound love for God may very well have been what caused his departure, body and soul, from this earth. Scripture says, "And Enoch walked with God; and he was not, for God took him" (Genesis 5:24 NKJV). Matthew Henry beautifully comments, "God showed how men should have left the world if they had not sinned, not by death, but by translation."

Are we walking so close to God that unbelievers recognize it? Their disfavor matters nothing if we're gaining God's favor instead.

The word of the LORD came expressly to Ezekiel the priest, the son of Buzi, in the land of the Chaldeans by the River Chebar; and the hand of the LORD was upon him there.

EZEKIEL 1:3 NKJV

Life can be anything but easy—and Ezekiel knew it, because he lived in one of Judah's most difficult times. The Assyrians had begun losing power to the rising Babylonian Empire, and Judah was stretched between the warring factions until Babylon conquered Jerusalem in 597 BC. That year, many Jews were exiled to Babylon, among them this son of a priest. In the new land, Ezekiel received the call to be a prophet.

Ezekiel's message wasn't a cheerful one. Unlike Jerusalem's false prophets, he told his exiled people that their time away from home would not be short—they'd better settle in. Jerusalem and the idolaters who remained there would be destroyed, and God's presence would leave the Temple.

Over and over, Ezekiel confronted the people with their sin and promised that judgment would follow. You can imagine that he wasn't the most popular man in town. Those who stand up to false prophets never get a lot of kudos, especially when they continually repeat the same cheerless message. Ezekiel's countrymen didn't like the message and often didn't listen to it.

But just about the time the people of Judah were

thoroughly tired of Ezekiel's message, God gave him another one. He spoke about the sins of Judah's neighbors and painted a picture of dry bones (all the Israelites) that would come back to Israel and serve God faithfully. Ezekiel saw a rebuilt Temple and God's glory returned to it. God's people would again own the land.

For twenty years, Ezekiel's ministry focused on sin and judgment. He probably got tired of it himself, but he faithfully repeated God's message until God chose to reveal His future plans. God had not deserted His people, though they were tempted to think so. In the right moment, Ezekiel reminded them of that fact.

When life does not seem easy and we don't have a cheerful message for others, are we still faithful? Or are we so caught up in the need for happiness that we can't accept the pain that life sometimes brings? Like Ezekiel, we need to speak clearly for our Lord and trust that He will bring the good news we've been seeking day by day.

*Ezra went up from Babylon; and he was a ready scribe
in the law of Moses, which the LORD God of Israel had given:
and the king granted him all his request, according to
the hand of the LORD his God upon him.*

EZRA 7:6 KJV

When King Darius I commanded Ezra to return to
Jerusalem and oversee the rebuilding of the Temple, he
wasn't offering the scribe-priest a cushy job. Ezra may have
had all the money and protection he needed from the
powerful Persian ruler, but plenty of trouble lay ahead.

A first wave of Temple rebuilders had returned to
Jerusalem when King Cyrus commanded the Temple to
be rebuilt in 538 BC. But succeeding kings had seen the
rebuilding project as a threat and had stopped it. Much
work lay ahead for Ezra.

When Ezra gathered his band of Israelites and priests
and had a prayer service to ask for God's protection on the
journey, he needed all the prayer he could get. Months later,
as he entered Jerusalem, he landed himself in big trouble.
Though the Israelites living in Babylon hadn't had an easy
life, at least they had been mindful of their background
and God's commands. Those remaining in Jerusalem had
become lax, to say the least.

Before Ezra had time to get his new home in order, the
reports were already in. The Israelite officials told the new
guy in town that many Jews, even priests, had intermarried

with the local pagan peoples. They expected Ezra to do something about the influence this had had on their nation. Not exactly the way to gain popularity in your homeland, was it? But Ezra didn't worry about that. He immediately turned to God in prayer, confessing the sins of his people and asking for forgiveness.

Graciously, God heard the priest's prayer and sent revival to His people. Those who had married apart from His Law put away their foreign spouses and returned to Him. Forgiveness covered the land.

When we face sudden, seemingly overwhelming troubles, do we worry about others' opinions, seek the counsel of the powerful, or begin by turning to God in prayer, believing He will act? Whether or not God responds immediately, His help is the first thing we need to seek. For when His grace intervenes, whatever its timing may be, our problems are solved.

GIDEON

*So [Gideon] said to Him, "O my Lord, how can I save Israel?
Indeed my clan is the weakest in Manasseh, and I
am the least in my father's house."*

JUDGES 6:15 NKJV

The biblical period recorded in the book of Judges is
perhaps the saddest in all of scripture. It stands in stark
contrast to the triumphant book of Joshua. We're told that
after the death of Joshua, another generation arose that
did not know the Lord or what He had done for Israel.
Instead, every man did what was right in his own eyes. Add
to this that Israel disobeyed God and had not eliminated
the heathen people of Canaan, and you have a recipe for
disaster.

In Gideon's days, all Israel was besieged by raiding
parties of Midianites and Amalekites, who stole across the
Jordan River to plunder food and whatever else they could
get their hands on. The Israelites hid their produce from
these raiders in dens and caves in the mountains. In such a
setting, Gideon had a heavenly encounter. While covertly
threshing wheat in his father's winepress, he was suddenly
greeted by an angel: "The LORD is with you, you mighty
man of valor!" (Judges 6:12 NKJV).

Stunned, Gideon managed to ask why Israel had fallen
victim to misfortune. When the angel told him that he
would be the one to liberate Israel from its oppressors,
Gideon was unnerved. Confessing the lowliness of his

father's clan, he also begged for a sign to confirm the angel's words. Accordingly, God built faith in Gideon by miraculously causing his offering to burn; He answered his requests for a wet or dry fleece; and then He allowed Gideon to hear the misgivings of his enemies (see Judges 6:19–22, 36–40; 7:8–14). What a comfort to know that God Almighty stoops paternally to strengthen us in our weakness.

God also performed a masterful "screening process" for Gideon's soldierly band, reducing their number to a mere three hundred men. He graciously informed Gideon as to why He did this (see Judges 7:2). Then, with his meager force armed only with trumpets, pitchers, and torches, Gideon, strengthened and guided by God, created deadly chaos in the enemy's camp, which led to a complete rout and total victory.

Time and time again in scripture, the children of Israel are told, "The battle is not yours; it is God's" (see Exodus 14:13–14; 2 Kings 6:8–16; 19:32–34; and 2 Chronicles 20:15, 17). Those words are just as true for us today as they were for Moses, Elisha, Hezekiah, Jehoshaphat, and Gideon. Can we respond with the same faith as these men?

GOLIATH

A champion named Goliath, who was from Gath,
came out of the Philistine camp. He was over nine feet tall.

1 SAMUEL 17:4

When the Israelites saw the massive Goliath and his impressive armor, their mouths must have gaped. It's not hard to understand why no one wanted to fight the huge Philistine champion. Who could win against a man with Goliath's battle experience and mighty weapons?

Only one Israelite believed he had a chance of winning. David, a shepherd boy who had defeated wild animals with his slingshot, saw Goliath as a wild man—one who had the nerve to defy God. The youth didn't think much about his opponent's size or armor; he was too busy thinking about his own powerful God.

David's confrontation with the giant made Goliath an example of "the bigger they are, the harder they fall." As David trusted God, his slingshot aimed accurately. A stone hit Goliath squarely in his forehead, and the huge fellow collapsed, dead. Quickly, David grabbed Goliath's giant sword and cut off the giant's head while the rest of the Philistines ran for their lives.

We may never have gone into battle, but we've faced our own giants. Do we throw in the towel, or do we follow in David's footsteps and trust God?

THE GOOD SAMARITAN

"But a Samaritan, as he traveled, came where the man was;
and when he saw him, he took pity on him."

LUKE 10:33

Scripture doesn't actually use the word *good* to describe
this Samaritan. And he wasn't an actual person, just a man
Jesus created in a parable. But his story has had a powerful
impact on people since the day our Lord told this tale.

The Good Samaritan came into being when a lawyer,
trying to find some wiggle room when Jesus told him to
love his neighbor, asked, "Who is my neighbor?" By the
end of Jesus' response, the legal beagle probably wished
he hadn't asked the question, for the Lord's answer has
challenged everyone who has ever heard the story. It doesn't
allow anyone to escape the harsh truth about the difficulty
of loving others.

Jesus told of a man who traveled from Jerusalem to
Jericho, a dangerous route along which robbers had easy
access to their victims. The innocent traveler was attacked,
beaten, and left for dead. As he lay in the road, others
passed him without helping. First, a priest walked by,
probably on the very far edge of the other side of the road.
What if the man is dead? he probably asked himself. *If I
touch him, I won't be able to do my priestly duty.* Or maybe
the religious leader was just too busy or didn't want to take
responsibility for a stranger.

Next, a Levite, one who acted as a priest's assistant,

came along, and he, too, avoided contaminating himself with the man in need. He probably shared the same concerns as the priest.

Left to these "religious" folk, the man in the road might have died. That's why God sent a Samaritan along. To the Israelites, Samaritans were particularly unsavory characters. After the Assyrians conquered Israel and deported much of the population, the conquerors repopulated the country with other peoples. The Samaritans' forebears were Jews who had intermarried with these pagans. Not only did this race have mixed blood, but they had also combined their faith in Yahweh, the God of Israel, with pagan religious practices. So the Samaritans were hated by the Jews on the basis of both their background and their beliefs.

But this "unholy" outlander had a heart of gold. When he saw the injured man, compassion filled his heart. He medicated and bandaged the hurting traveler, placed him on his donkey, and carried him to the closest inn. There he paid the bill and promised the innkeeper more money for caring for the stranger.

Following this brief tale, which never tells us what ultimately happened to the traveler, Jesus asked the lawyer which of the three passersby was a neighbor to the hurting man. Perhaps constrained by his distaste from pronouncing the hated name *Samaritan*, the lawyer answered, "The one who had mercy on him."

"Go and do likewise," Jesus commanded.

The Samaritan's tale challenges us not to become so caught up in the legalities of faith that our hearts turn cold.

Like the religious leaders who passed by on the wrong side, it's easy for us to get wrapped up in our own lives and ignore those in need. But Christian faith requires that we not only tell people about Jesus, but live out the kind of faith that makes Him real to others.

Are we up to the Good Samaritan's challenge? Only if Jesus fills our hearts each day!

HEROD

After Jesus was born in Bethlehem in Judea, during the time of King Herod, Magi from the east came to Jerusalem and asked, "Where is the one who has been born king of the Jews? We saw his star in the east and have come to worship him." When King Herod heard this he was disturbed.

MATTHEW 2:1–3

When Herod the Great wasn't happy, nobody else was either. Unhappy with his sons, he murdered a few—even his favorites. As Emperor Augustus declared, it was better to be Herod's pig than his son.

This paranoid king exterminated anyone who threatened his authority. That's why, when he heard about Jesus' birth, he killed all the young boys in Bethlehem. But while he tore people down, Herod was known for his building projects— he began work on rebuilding the Temple and erected pagan altars and many public buildings.

When Herod died, three of his sons inherited his lands. Herod Antipas, who governed Galilee and Perea, became involved in the Jewish dispute that led to Jesus' death.

Herod the Great spent his life worrying about losing power. Do we also worry about the things of this world at the expense of eternity? No one remembers Herod's building projects, but even well-read non-Christians can tell you he murdered his sons and innocent children.

HEZEKIAH

Hezekiah trusted in the LORD, the God of Israel.
There was no one like him among all the kings of Judah,
either before him or after him.

2 KINGS 18:5

Scripture never tells us how a son of wicked King Ahab of Judah became a faithful believer. But at age twenty-five, Hezekiah came to power, removed the pagan places of worship from his land, and destroyed false objects of worship.

Scripture praises Hezekiah highly for his faithfulness. His walk was a consistent one, unlike those of many other rulers of his age. God blessed him for this, making him successful in his rebellion against the king of Assyria and in battle with the Philistines. But in the fourteenth year of Hezekiah's reign, King Sennacherib of Assyria captured

Judah's fortified cities and sent his military counselor to talk Hezekiah into admitting defeat. Though Hezekiah gave the powerful king a huge tribute, it was not enough. Sennacherib wanted Hezekiah out of office. So an Assyrian military commander came with a message and even tried to sway the men of Jerusalem with dark warnings of what would happen if they held out against his master.

Judah's king knew where to go in times of trouble. He immediately dressed in sackcloth, indicating his spiritual humility, and sent two men straight to the prophet Isaiah. The prophet offered the king encouraging news: Sennacherib would hear a rumor that would send him quickly home. When Sennacherib's commander returned, he denigrated the power of Hezekiah's God. Judah's king turned to God in prayer, placing all his fears before the Lord. Again Isaiah prophesied that Jerusalem would not be hurt.

That night, 185,000 men in the Assyrian camp died at the hand of the angel of the Lord. Sennacherib returned to his home and was killed there by two of his sons.

Then, scripture tells us, Hezekiah became deathly ill. Isaiah warned him to prepare for death, but the king prayed again, and God gave him fifteen more years of life and promised to protect his city.

The king of Babylon sent envoys to Hezekiah, who proudly showed off his wealth to them. Perhaps Judah's king wanted to impress the Babylonians, but instead he gave them other ideas. After the envoys returned home, Isaiah prophesied that all Hezekiah had shown them would be taken to Babylon in a coming exile. The king was simply thankful it would not happen in his lifetime.

When Hezekiah faced problems, he didn't worry. He became a prayer warrior. Do we do likewise, placing our cares firmly in the hands of the Almighty, trusting He will save us? Then we, too, are faithful Hezekiahs, who may hear God's praise for our lives.

HOSEA

When the LORD began to speak through Hosea,
the LORD said to him, "Go, take to yourself an adulterous
wife and children of unfaithfulness, because the land is
guilty of the vilest adultery in departing from the LORD."

HOSEA 1:2

Could God really have commanded His prophet to marry a prostitute? Scholars disagree. Some say it really happened, while others maintain that Hosea had a vision so real that it was as if it had really occurred. But scripture recounts the story as fact.

In the northern kingdom of Israel, Baal worship had been combined with worship of God. Hosea lived in the midst of this syncretism, with people who added pagan practices on top of a biblical faith and didn't seem to think that God would mind. The book of Hosea depicts these events as a family split by marital infidelity.

Daily, Hosea stood in the middle of the division between real faith and paganism. In his own family life, he lived on the fault line of unbelief and real faith. Scholars who believe the story is literal conjecture that Hosea's first child was his own, but the following two were the result of his wife's unfaithfulness. This wasn't an ideal marriage by any means. But it's God's honest picture of what His relationship with Israel was really like.

Hosea tenderly describes God's love and the pain His people's unfaithfulness brought Him. Even as, through the prophet, God promised judgment, He wooed His beloved ones back with a promise of mercy.

God commanded Hosea to love Gomer, a woman who did not love him in return. When she left him, he was sent by God to bring her back into his life. Though his wife had run to a lover, Hosea bought her out of slavery and gently directed her to remain faithful to him. Like Gomer, Israel had been drawn away by the sinful attractions of neighboring countries. To most of Israel, the fertility god Baal looked more pleasing than the Lord. But the Israelites were running themselves toward destruction. Their kings sold out to the pagan kings of Assyria, looking there for protection instead of to God. Israel had sown the wind and would reap the whirlwind (see Hosea 8:7). Yet the Lord warned them of the coming danger and called them back to Himself.

Though God repeatedly chastised His people, He did not end the book of Hosea in judgment, but by again calling His unrepentant people back to Himself.

Have you ever doubted that God really loves you? Read the book of Hosea. Could anyone on earth forgive you that much, want you that much, and be that patient with you? Maybe you'll never love anyone that way, under your own power, but God can empower you with His unending love.

THE IMMORAL MAN OF CORINTH

It is actually reported that there is sexual immorality among you, and of a kind that does not occur even among pagans: A man has his father's wife.

1 CORINTHIANS 5:1

We often assume that most Christians won't engage in the "big sins." Sure, we all struggle with something, but sexual immorality of the sort Paul describes here shocks us as much as it did the fertility-god-worshipping Greeks.

All sorts of sinful behavior may go on, even within the church. But it usually happens behind closed doors; and when it's unearthed, woe to the sinner! Yet in Corinth, the whole congregation knew that one man was having sexual encounters with "his father's wife," believed by many Bible teachers to be the man's stepmother—but no one intervened to rebuke the sinner. So Paul came down hard on the whole church.

These relatively new Christians deserved the rebuke. Everyone in Corinth was no doubt gossiping, "Did you hear what's going on over there in the First Corinthian Church? They enjoy incest!" The congregation's witness had been damaged. So Paul insisted that the Corinthians toss out the man who had sinned in order to make things right.

It may seem hard on the sinner to toss him out summarily, but if we're wise, we won't condone sin in our churches or in our lives. Better to toss one man out than to have others caught up in the same sin. A repentant sinner can always return, but ignoring sin will ruin Christians and their churches.

ISAAC

"Your wife Sarah will bear you a son, and you will call him Isaac. I will establish my covenant with him as an everlasting covenant for his descendants after him."

GENESIS 17:19

If good things are worth waiting for, Isaac must have been wonderful. His parents received the promise of his birth twenty-five years before his birthday. When they heard his first cry, how excited Abraham and Sarah must have been! Here, after all these years, was their covenant child of promise.

To protect him, the couple made Isaac's jealous half

brother, Ishmael, and his mother, Hagar, leave their camp so that nothing would threaten God's gift. Sarah had tried to lend God a helping hand and had given her maid to Abraham to have a child for her. Now Ishmael was a terrible problem and had to be gotten rid of.

Then God asked Abraham to sacrifice Isaac on an altar. As father and son drew near to the place of sacrifice, Isaac realized that they lacked an animal to place on the altar. God would provide it, Abraham promised. Yet suddenly, Isaac found himself on top of the altar, and his father had a knife in his hand. How both must have rejoiced when they heard the bleat of that ram in the thicket and knew that God had provided. Perhaps Isaac wiped his brow with relief. No doubt the word *salvation* had new meaning for him.

We next hear of Isaac when Abraham arranged a marriage for his forty-year-old son, sending a servant back to his homeland to seek a bride. The servant returned with a dream girl, Abraham's grandniece Rebekah, and Isaac loved her.

But when the babies didn't come, Isaac prayed for a child. That must have been some prayer, for God gave the couple twins—Esau and Jacob. Esau was his father's darling, but the favored son easily sold his birthright to Jacob. Then Rebekah plotted with Jacob to gain Isaac's blessing, which would give Jacob authority over the family. Jacob's successful bid for power forced him to flee Esau's wrath. Many years would pass before he returned and made peace with his brother. But at least he was there when his aged father died.

God's faithfulness shines through Isaac's life. God promised Abraham a son, and though he was a long time coming, Isaac was born, and he trusted in the Lord. The incident in which he almost became a sacrifice did not separate Isaac from God. No turn of life broke his faith. Isaac held fast to the Lord.

Can others say the same of us?

ISAIAH

The vision concerning Judah and Jerusalem
that Isaiah son of Amoz saw during the reigns of Uzziah,
Jotham, Ahaz and Hezekiah, kings of Judah.

ISAIAH 1:1

The four kings who heard Isaiah's prophetic messages may have been hearing God's word to them from a relative. Some scholars believe that Isaiah was the nephew of Judah's King Amaziah. Yet the prophet didn't hold back. He offered a straightforward and less-than-pleasing message: Judah had rebelled against God and offended Him at every turn.

Isaiah worked in an age of political instability. He took up his prophetic mantle in 739 BC, the year King Uzziah died. During the monarchies of Uzziah and Jotham, the militaristic Assyrian Empire had ignored the tiny countries to its southeast. But during Ahaz's reign, a succession of Assyrian kings expanded their empire in the direction of Judah.

Israel and Syria begged Judah to join them in repelling the encroaching nation. They didn't take Ahaz's refusal well and fought him. As other nations opportunistically attacked Judah and Ahaz's power began to crumble, he called on Assyria to support him. It did. Israel was vanquished by the Assyrians in 722 BC, and Judah became a vassal state. Still, things did not go well for Ahaz. Assyria intended to have Judah under its own control, not his. Instead of turning to God, Ahaz followed the Assyrians into open idolatry. He closed the Temple and removed its valuable objects.

When Isaiah prophesied to Ahaz, his messages combined encouragement with predictions of future destruction for Judah's opponents. Yet Ahaz ignored the prophet and became a thoroughgoing pagan. He was so bad that when he died, his people would not bury him with Judah's other kings.

Though Isaiah's book records many messages that God spoke through him, and we know the history of the kings, scripture does not tell us much about the prophet himself. His glorious prophecies, filled with information about the coming Messiah and a deep understanding of God's nature, indicate that he was a man of extremely deep faith.

Yet only a few chapters in 2 Kings show the prophet in action. In 701 BC, under King Hezekiah, Judah rebelled against Assyria. King Sennacherib, determined to take command over the nation, conquered Judah's outlying fortresses and sent a messenger to Jerusalem with an ultimatum: Give up.

Faced with the threat of annihilation, faithful Hezekiah called upon the Lord and sent his men for Isaiah. The prophet promised that Sennacherib would return to his own country, leaving Judah whole, and that Sennacherib would be killed in his homeland. Quickly, Hezekiah received a message that confirmed the first part of that promise.

Relieved and thankful, Hezekiah praised God for the deliverance, and God heard the king's prayer. That night, He took the lives of 185,000 Assyrian soldiers, and the rest of the army fled for home. There Sennacherib's sons killed him.

Hezekiah must have been a powerful man of prayer, for scripture tells us of a time when he was ill. Isaiah broke the bad news: The king would not recover. But Hezekiah wept before God, and the Lord extended his life by fifteen years. Isaiah reported that good news and God's promise to protect Jerusalem from the king of Assyria. As a sign, the prophet moved a shadow back ten steps.

When the king of Babylon sent envoys to Hezekiah, he showed off all his treasures. In the final prophecy ascribed to Isaiah, he had the sad job of telling Hezekiah that all he'd shown off would be carried away to Babylon. But it would happen during the reign of one of his sons, not while faithful Hezekiah was still alive.

According to tradition, and possibly alluded to in scripture (see Hebrews 11:37), Isaiah was eventually put to death by being sawn in two.

Isaiah's messages are filled with colorful imagery, a vital

understanding of God, and a clear vision of the Lord's plan for His people. The prophet drew close to God and gained an awesome depth of understanding from his faithful walk with Him. In a dangerous time, he spoke clearly and honestly to a people who did not want to hear him.

Wouldn't we all like to be faithful like Isaiah?

JACOB

Jacob said to his father, "I am Esau your firstborn.
I have done as you told me. Please sit up and eat some
of my game so that you may give me your blessing."

GENESIS 27:19

Before Jacob and Esau were born, God promised that the older twin would serve the younger—a backward situation in that culture and time. But God didn't stop there. He continued blessing Jacob, the younger son, over his disobedient older brother, even though the chosen Jacob often lived a less-than-perfect life.

As the twins grew, Jacob became the home-loving son, while brother Esau turned into an outdoorsman. Though Jacob was his mama Rebekah's favorite, his father, Isaac, favored Esau. One day, when Isaac was old, weak, and nearly blind, he asked Esau to hunt some game and make him a meal. In return, he'd bless his most-loved son, ignoring God's promise.

Rebekah overheard the conversation, warned Jacob, and came up with a plot. Jacob would pretend to be his brother. Having his mother make up a goat stew and covering himself in goat hair worked: Isaac gave him dominion over Esau.

But now Jacob had to deal with his brother—a very angry man who was ready to commit murder. For Jacob's safety, Rebekah convinced Isaac to send her favorite son on a visit to Uncle Laban, to find a bride. During the journey, Jacob had a dream in which God promised to bless him. But the deceiver was about to receive a taste of his own medicine. No sooner had he neared Laban's neighborhood than Jacob met his cousin Rachel and fell head-over-heels in love with her. He promised his uncle that he would work seven years for his bride. But Laban's older, less beautiful daughter, Leah, needed to marry first. So on the wedding night, crafty Laban slipped the wrong woman into Jacob's tent. By morning, the young man could do nothing but admit that he had a wife he didn't want and negotiate a new deal to get Rachel.

So Jacob began a life that denied God's plan. To gain Rachel, he worked another seven years for his uncle. Meanwhile, Leah began bearing him children—while Rachel remained barren—and a competition started between the sisters. Desperate to provide a son for Jacob, Rachel gave him her maid to bear children for her. Then Leah gave her maid to Jacob, as well. Before long, Jacob had more women than he could handle, and they kept adding to the family. By the end, Jacob had twelve sons and a daughter. Conflict must have filled the camp until Jacob felt like leaving. Instead, he set himself up to gain a large herd of livestock, making a deal with Laban that he twisted to his own advantage. Yet despite his conniving nature, Jacob was blessed by God.

Then Jacob took his family and moved toward his homeland. And God renamed him Israel.

Israel's reunion with Esau was surprisingly uneventful. But at Shechem, his daughter, Dinah, was raped by the son of the ruler. Two of Israel's sons, Simeon and Levi, all but started a war over the issue, so Israel and his family and flocks moved on to Bethel. There God gave Israel His covenant promise, and he built an altar.

Just about the time that Israel might have felt things were settling down, his older sons sold off his favorite son, Joseph, Rachel's firstborn, and sorrow filled the camp. For years, Israel didn't know what really happened, until a drought came and he sent his sons into Egypt for provisions. There they discovered that the brother they thought was dead was now the second most powerful man in Egypt.

At Joseph's request, Israel and his family traveled to Egypt, where Joseph could care for them. Israel blessed his sons before he died in Egypt and made them promise to return his body to their homeland. Joseph had his father's body embalmed and returned to his homeland to fulfill that promise.

Though Jacob had seasons in which he obeyed God less than perfectly, God never changed in His purpose or commitment. He never abandoned Israel. Though we may find ourselves in baffling situations that turn out in ways we never expected, God will never give up on us, either, as we seek His will.

JAMES, BROTHER OF JESUS

"Isn't this the carpenter? Isn't this Mary's son and the brother of James, Joseph, Judas and Simon? Aren't his sisters here with us?" And they took offense at him.

MARK 6:3

When the truth that Jesus was more than an ordinary man suddenly hit the people of Nazareth, they were astounded. How could He be more than an everyday fellow? After all, wasn't He just like His brother James? An admirable person maybe, but nothing more.

The truth is, at first James didn't believe in his half brother's claims either. Perhaps he couldn't get away from His teaching, but that didn't mean he had to agree with Jesus.

But a change came over James. In the book of Acts, he appears as a church leader: He spoke for the Jerusalem council that heard Paul's objections to circumcision for the Gentiles, and Paul reported to that council on his missionary experience when he returned to Jerusalem.

James probably wrote the biblical book that bears his

name, which is filled with guidance for living an effective Christian life. Within the early church, he was known as James the Just because of his upright character. He was martyred in AD 62, after being thrown down from the Temple.

As we've come to know Jesus and have seen His power, have we had a change of heart like the one James had, from unbelief to faith?

JAMES, SON OF ZEBEDEE

James son of Zebedee and his brother John (to them he gave the name Boanerges, which means Sons of Thunder.

MARK 3:17

While James and his brother, John, quietly mended their fishing nets, Jesus called them to become fishers of men. These two hotheads—"Sons of Thunder," Jesus called them—didn't stop to think; they simply jumped out of the boat and ran to the Master. But it was the best quick decision they'd ever made. The two went from being part of a family business to becoming key members in the family of God.

James and John became part of the inner circle of Jesus' most trusted disciples. James was there when Jesus healed Simon Peter's mother and when He quietly raised Jairus's daughter from the dead. Only Peter, James, and John witnessed the second event. There must have been a special trust between these men and their Lord.

The same three disciples saw Jesus' clothing turn bright white and heard Him speak to Elijah and Moses on the Mount of Transfiguration. Stunned by this preview of Jesus' eternal glory, the three hardly knew what to make of it. But they trustingly kept the secret when Jesus commanded them to.

As Jesus headed to Jerusalem for the final time, He stopped in a less-than-welcoming Samaritan village. When James and his brother discovered the town's attitude, they suggested a fine Christian response: "Let's command fire to come down and wipe out these folks." Jesus, of course, rebuked these two, who still had a long way to walk in their faith.

In Jerusalem, the brothers' mother, Salome, had a request: She wanted Jesus to give her sons places right beside Him in His kingdom. Perhaps she had overheard her sons discussing one of the Twelve's favorite topics: Who was greatest among them? Wasn't this the ultimate in seeing her sons succeed in their work?

When Jesus responded by asking whether they could drink the cup He was about to drink, James and John confidently asserted they could. No doubters, these two, in their own powers.

Finally, in the Garden of Gethsemane, the three trusted disciples heard Jesus' prayers as He prepared for His great sacrifice. Yet James's name is missing from the accounts of the Crucifixion. Though we're told that John and Salome stood by watching, neither James nor Peter is mentioned.

We next hear of James in Acts 12:2, when Herod Agrippa puts him to death by the sword.

Confident and brash, perhaps James doesn't seem perfect apostle material. But God called him, and he followed determinedly, despite his failings. God uses all personalities, the brash and the timid, to do His work, if only we'll follow Him.

JEREMIAH

The words of Jeremiah the son of Hilkiah,
of the priests who were in Anathoth in the land of Benjamin,
to whom the word of the LORD came in the days
of Josiah the son of Amon, king of Judah.

JEREMIAH 1:1–2 NKJV

Jeremiah is known as Judah's "weeping prophet," and he had a lot to cry about, as you'll see if you read his prophecies and the book of Lamentations. He spoke to people who refused to listen to his message—God's last-ditch effort to reach the nation of Judah before destruction fell upon them. Called to his ministry while still young, Jeremiah never married; instead, he single-mindedly conveyed God's call to repentance for more than forty years.

Assyria, which had conquered Israel, was the first to fall to the Chaldeans of Babylon. The conflict between these two superpowers left Judah to prosper under good

King Josiah. When Josiah died in battle against Assyria's allies, the Egyptians, Jeremiah lamented the loss of the king. Egypt transported Josiah's son Jehoahaz and made his brother Jehoiakim king.

In 612 BC, the Babylonians conquered Assyria and began building an empire. Jeremiah started warning his rebellious people of their dangerous future. Babylonian King Nebuchadnezzar invaded, and Jehoiakim became his vassal. But three years later, he rebelled. Following a tumultuous eleven-year rule, wicked Jehoiakim died, and his young son, Jehoiachin, took his throne. In just over three months, Nebuchadnezzar replaced Jehoiachin with the evil Zedekiah.

Life must have become nearly unbearable for Jeremiah as the new king, the officers of the priests, and the people were all unfaithful. Zedekiah rebelled against Nebuchadnezzar, who retaliated by attacking Jerusalem. After the Babylonians suddenly withdrew, Jeremiah was called a traitor to his people and imprisoned until a eunuch in the king's household came to his aid.

Nebuchadnezzar retaliated for Judah's rebellion by burning both the city and the Temple of Jerusalem and killing all of Zedekiah's sons and nobles. The king's life was spared, but his eyes were put out and he was taken captive to Babylon. Jeremiah, too, was delivered from death, and he was eventually taken to Egypt when his people fled there against his advice. He most likely died while in Egypt.

Though he struggled greatly and was deeply hurt by both kings and common people, Jeremiah remained ever faithful to his unchanging God. His situation did not set the agenda for belief or action. Instead, his faith determined all he believed and did. When our lives are troubled, do we follow in Jeremiah's faithful footsteps?

JESUS

Jesus said to them, "My food is to do the will of Him who sent Me, and to finish His work."

JOHN 4:34 NKJV

Where do we start in talking about Jesus? After all, didn't the apostle John say that if everything Jesus did was written down, the world couldn't contain all the books about Him? What better place to begin than with what He Himself considered foundational. Numerous times throughout the Gospels, Jesus refers to "Him who sent Me." Keenly aware of the mission He had been sent to accomplish, Jesus was also wholeheartedly committed to the One who had sent Him.

To accomplish His Father's will, Jesus had to vindicate His Father's glory, which Satan had hopelessly tried to usurp. Yes, Jesus came to atone for sin, but His greatest objective was to perfectly glorify His Father. Jesus was determined to show the entire universe that, contrary to Satan's claims, God the Father was still holy, just, and righteous. The achievement of this objective culminated in Jesus' crucifixion, death, and resurrection.

Do we have the slightest inkling what it took for Jesus to live with such precision? Among other things, He had to perfectly fulfill the entire Law that God had given to Moses—and He was the only One who ever did. Aside from that, He had to fulfill all the messianic prophecies. John the Baptist was aghast to see Jesus coming forward to be baptized. "I need to be baptized by You, and are You coming to me?" he said. But Jesus replied, "Permit it to be so now, for thus it is fitting for us to fulfill all righteousness" (Matthew 3:14–15 NKJV). Jesus didn't have to be baptized, because He'd never sinned. Still, He went ahead with the rite in order to qualify as *the* Sin Bearer.

Surely, Satan did everything he could to trip Jesus up. Just after Jesus' baptism, scripture says He was led away by the Holy Spirit into the desert. While there, Jesus fasted for forty days, after which He was hungry. Satan seized upon this opportunity to tempt Jesus. Three times, the evil one tried by appealing to need, greed, and ego—all basic human drives. Yet for each temptation Jesus had but one weapon—the Word of God. He would not be hindered from accomplishing the Father's will, no matter what Satan hurled at Him.

A large part of Jesus' accomplishment of the Father's will had to do with His selecting and cultivating twelve ordinary men to be His apostles. This was a real test for Jesus. Unlike Him, all of them had their faults and weaknesses, and one of them would actually betray Him.

If that weren't enough, Jesus had only three short years in which to prepare these men to become His leading ambassadors. If ever we're tempted to feel as if we don't measure up in Jesus' eyes, we need look no further than the apostles for perspective. Here was a group of imperfect men, all too often seeking their own will instead of God's. Even so, Jesus patiently bore with them and never once gave up on them, even on that fateful night at Gethsemane when they all abandoned Him.

Gethsemane was Jesus' next to worst test. His worst was when the Father turned His back on Him as He hung on the cross. Jesus became sin on that cross, sinking lower than any human being ever had or ever will. The Father, repelled by sin, could not bear to look upon His Son. Driven to despair, Jesus cried out, "My God, My God, why have You forsaken Me?" (Matthew 27:46 NKJV). Then came the triumph of all triumphs. Jesus knew He had carried out the Father's will to the very last and said, "It is finished!" More beautiful words of liberation could not be spoken.

Jesus' weapon against Satan is our weapon, as well. Let us never forget that God's Word is all we need to seek, know, and do for His will to become our own. It is also all we need to repel the fiery darts that Satan hurls at us.

*In the land of Uz there lived a man whose name was Job.
This man was blameless and upright;
he feared God and shunned evil.*

JOB 1:1

Why do bad things happen to great believers? Job wondered.
He'd spent his life trying to follow God, making the
right sacrifices, putting his spiritual life first. But one day,
everything seemed to fall apart. Job went from owning
thousands of livestock and having a happy family to losing
it all. Oxen, donkeys, sheep, and camels were stolen or
killed. Before the messengers who brought the news could
finish their tales, another came to tell Job that all his
children had died when the house had been destroyed by a
terrible wind.

Yet Job worshipped God.

Sores erupted on his whole body. Still, he held firmly to
his integrity, though his less-than-supportive wife suggested
that he curse God and die.

Three of Job's friends came to comfort him. For a week
they sat, mouths closed. What could they say to a faithful
man who had suffered so deeply? When they finally started
talking, Job probably wished he could gag them. Perplexed
by his troubles, they quickly came to the conclusion that
Job had sinned. Why else would God punish him? Job
contended with them as they yammered on and on about
the impossibility of his innocence. As Job speaks, we get a

clear picture of the physical, spiritual, and emotional pain that dogged him.

Just when the three might have been winding down, Elihu, a young man, joined in the abuse. Though he glorifies God, like the other less-than-comforting comforters, he also ends up condemning Job.

Finally, God intervenes and answers Job in a strange way. He does not explain that the events came about because He was showing Satan Job's faithfulness. Instead, the Lord gives Job a glorious picture of His power and authority. Job is silenced. As God continues, Job admits his own ignorance and repents.

God rebukes the comfortless comforters. He orders them to make a sacrifice of repentance and promises that Job will pray for them.

God gave Job back all that he had lost—new flocks and a new family. But the best part of this new life was probably Job's new, deeper relationship with the Lord. He could trust Him, no matter what came into his life, for God was infinitely greater than he'd imagined.

When we face trials, will we remember the God who revealed Himself to Job and place our entire future in His hands?

JOEL

The word of the LORD that came to Joel son of Pethuel.

JOEL 1:1

We really don't know a lot about Joel, or even about his book of the Bible, beyond the evidence it gives about itself.

Because Joel does not mention his country or king, we cannot date his book with precision. He is largely concerned with Jerusalem, so he was probably from Judah, but scholars have differed on the time in which he lived. Joel uses language typical of all the prophets, so using linguistic methods to date his book has not proved successful.

Joel reports the desolation of the land by locusts and invaders. Desperation fills the people, and the prophet calls for repentance. Then he pictures the day of the Lord, both in the immediate sense, as his people are attacked, and the long-term vision in which the Lord will judge all nations. One day, as pagan nations are judged, God's people will be restored. In either case, Joel encourages God's people to trust in Him as their refuge. His book ends with the words "The LORD dwells in Zion" (Joel 3:21).

Whether disaster or blessing overcomes us, do we believe that God remains on His throne and rules our lives?

*When [Jesus] had gone a little farther, he saw James son
of Zebedee and his brother John in a boat, preparing their
nets. Without delay he called them, and they left their father
Zebedee in the boat with the hired men and followed him.*

MARK 1:19–20

When Jesus called John to be His disciple, He had to have
a lot of imagination about His new follower, who probably
had more of a reputation for his temper than his holiness.
John and his older brother, James, came from a family that
owned their own fishing business. Things must have gone
well for Zebedee, because he employed not only James and
John, but also some hired hands.

Perhaps success is why the sons of Zebedee were
used to having things their own way: They certainly had
commanding personalities. When the disciples met a man
who was driving demons out in the Master's name, John
planned to stop him in his tracks. After all, the stranger
wasn't one of *them*. Later, when a small village didn't take
kindly to having Jesus and His twelve disciples take shelter
with them, James and John wanted to call down fire on
these people. The brothers' fiery tempers earned them a
nickname from Jesus: *Boanerges*, which means "Sons of
Thunder."

Despite his short fuse, John became Jesus' dearest
disciple. Jesus called him, along with James and Peter, to
witness key events such as the healings of Peter's mother

and Jairus's daughter, the Transfiguration, and Jesus' prayer in the Garden of Gethsemane. Scholars also generally believe that "the disciple Jesus loved," who is referred to in John's Gospel and experiences some of the most crucial moments in that book, is John himself.

John's Gospel and epistles show an intense, passionate love relationship with God. Along with Peter and James, John experiences some of scripture's most intimate spiritual moments with the Savior. And the biblical books that bear his name show a deep, tender understanding of the Master. His Gospel relates incidents that do not appear in the other Gospels. But as he neared the end of his life, John had become humble. In his Gospel, he never tells of his own call by Jesus or overemphasizes his own role in the spread of the good news.

Yet clearly the humble disciple had a key place in the gospel mission: Because John knew Caiaphas, the high priest, he and Peter got to view and report on Jesus' trial. At the Crucifixion, Jesus gave His mother into John's care. And Mary Magdalene came to John and Peter to report the disappearance of Jesus' body.

As the church grew, John stood by his friend Peter when Peter healed a beggar in the Temple gate. Together, the friends were arrested by the authorities and firmly declared their intention to continue spreading God's message of His Son.

John's epistles to the church do not name him as their writer. The early church fathers record his relationship to these letters. First John encourages believers and gives them the tools to fight against the heresy of Gnosticism. His practical advice must have been a real boon to the church in a turbulent age. The following two smaller books are personal letters that give us insight into the Christian life in his era and into the relationships John had with others. John's most stunning book is his prophecy of the last times, Revelation. As the nascent church struggled to exist, John envisioned a glorious future in which Jesus will rule eternally, victorious over sin and earthly tyrants.

With his church, John suffered persecution. Near the end of his life, he was exiled to the island of Patmos, where he wrote Revelation, but tradition has it that he returned to his ministry in Ephesus and died of old age. He is the only apostle not to have been martyred.

Because John was willing to follow his Lord faithfully, God took a firebrand and made him into a humble apostle. Not every firebrand does the same, but God seems to use a fair number of them. Struggle with your temper? Don't forget what God can do. Give Him authority, and He can turn you sweet with love for Him.

JOHN THE BAPTIST

*[John said,]"He must increase,
but I must decrease."*

JOHN 3:30 NKJV

When John the Baptist arrived on the scene, four hundred years of prophetic silence came to a crashing end. From out of nowhere, this electric figure hastened upon the scene, full of energy and conviction. No knight in shining armor astride a mighty steed, but a rough, desert-hewn figure in coarse clothing, wielding the very word of God. The Messiah's herald had finally come like a whirlwind out of the desert, "in the spirit and power of Elijah" (Luke 1:17 NKJV).

To be in the company of John the Baptist was to live in a charged air of immanency concerning this Anointed One of God called the Messiah. In centuries long past, the prophets had predicted His coming. The angel of the Lord had even given the prophet Daniel a timeline pinpointing the Messiah's arrival (see Daniel 9:20–27). If Messiah did not come within that timeline, He would not come at all!

In light of this, John's message to the people of Israel was urgent and uncompromising. "Repent, for the kingdom of heaven is at hand! . . . Even now the ax is laid to the root of the trees. Therefore every tree which does not bear good fruit is cut down and thrown into the fire" (Matthew 3:2, 10 NKJV). This John proclaimed to all, whether they listened or not. To underscore his words,

John controversially adapted an existing ritual—baptism. Baptism was the norm for converts to Judaism, but those who were already Jews? God imposed a new requirement for cleansing, and the people came willingly to be baptized. Even Jesus subjected Himself to this requirement, "to fulfill all righteousness" (Matthew 3:15 NKJV). So serious was John about this matter that, when he saw Pharisees and Sadducees approaching to be baptized, he exploded, "Brood of vipers! Who warned you to flee from the wrath to come? Therefore bear fruits worthy of repentance, and do not think to say to yourselves, 'We have Abraham as our father.' For I say to you that God is able to raise up children to Abraham from these stones" (Matthew 3:7–9 NKJV). With these words, John destroyed all self-importance forever!

John the Baptist had a mission, and he clearly understood it. Asked by the priests and Levites who he was, he answered, "I am 'The voice of one crying in the wilderness: "Make straight the way of the LORD," ' as the prophet Isaiah said" (John 1:23 NKJV). Pressed further about his baptizing, John said, "I baptize with water, but there stands One among you whom you do not know. It is He who, coming after me, is preferred before me, whose sandal strap I am not worthy to loose" (John 1:26–27 NKJV). "I indeed baptize you with water unto repentance, but He who is coming after me is mightier than I, whose sandals I am not worthy to carry. He will baptize you with the Holy Spirit and fire" (Matthew 3:11 NKJV).

By virtue of the Holy Spirit, John understood he was but the forerunner of One far greater than he, and he was content with that. He also understood his limitations and knew that the One coming after him was vested with powers and abilities far beyond his own. John was preparing the people for and pointing them to Jesus. While languishing in Herod's prison, he sent his disciples to Jesus to hear from His own mouth that neither they nor John need look for anyone else but Him.

Prior to his arrest, John humbly acknowledged that it was time for him to step aside to allow Jesus to take center stage. "Therefore this joy of mine is fulfilled. He must increase, but I must decrease" (John 3:29–30 NKJV).

In this day of "Me first!" it would seem that very few men are content to play second fiddle. Those who want the spotlight will usually do anything they can to get it. Not so with John the Baptist. He understood who Jesus was. Not until we ourselves understand who Jesus really is will we be able to step aside like John and let Jesus reign in our lives.

JONAH

But Jonah arose to flee to Tarshish
from the presence of the LORD.

JONAH 1:3 NKJV

Well now, here is a man who didn't need to be taught prejudice. For Jonah, it was only natural to hate the wicked city-state called Nineveh.

Ironically, the name Nineveh means "agreeable dwelling." The city itself is believed to have been a marvel. Scripture refers to it as "that great city" (Jonah 1:2 NKJV). It was surrounded by high walls and numerous watchtowers. In Jonah's day, Nineveh's earthly defenses were unparalleled. Inside the city, there was an array of buildings and palaces, the decor of which would rival that of any other great city of its time. Nineveh's commerce and industry were thriving and without comparison.

Yet for all its splendor and magnificence, Nineveh was an abomination in the eyes of God. He told Jonah, "Arise, go to Nineveh, that great city, and cry out against it; for their wickedness has come up before Me" (Jonah 1:2 NKJV). Wait a minute! A Hebrew prophet being sent to preach to a heathen city, and the archenemy of Israel to boot? Unheard of!

What sort of wickedness could have aroused God's wrath? For one thing, Nineveh was a center of excess where common, ordinary, everyday folks didn't matter. Drunkenness and sexual immorality of the vilest sort were rampant. Most any sort of crime or vice prospered within its walls. Sound familiar?

If this weren't enough, the Assyrians weren't known for their compassion toward conquered people. If anything, they were ruthless and barbaric in their treatment, as evidenced by the mounds of skulls that served as "monuments" to their conquests. Aside from all this, they didn't care much for either Judah or Israel. In fact, they would have much preferred to make both kingdoms a vast tract of rubble.

No wonder Jonah wasn't too keen on going to Nineveh. It's quite likely that Jonah himself could have been a victim of Assyrian cruelty as a result of one of their military ventures into Israel. That would have only reinforced his hatred for Nineveh and cemented his decision to disobey God.

When God finally did get the prophet's attention, after turning him into fish bait, Jonah resolutely set out for Nineveh. Getting the Ninevites' attention wasn't any great trouble for Jonah, for he was a sight—and smell—to behold! He drew crowds in Nineveh, but they no doubt kept him at arm's length, holding their noses. Word reached the king about this conversation piece who was proclaiming a dire message of unalterable doom. Then to Jonah's amazement and disgust, all the people of Nineveh, as well as all their animals, donned sackcloth and ashes, and the people prayed for God to relent.

Jonah knew God's mercy. He said, "For I know that You are a gracious and merciful God, slow to anger and abundant in lovingkindness, One who relents from doing harm" (Jonah 4:2 NKJV). Even so, Jonah wished that

Nineveh had perished in perdition.

Where or what are the Ninevehs in our lives? Are they cities or places we can't stand, the very mention of whose names makes us bristle? Are they perhaps sports teams we just love to hate? Who might the Ninevites be in our lives? Are they folks with a particular philosophy or bent that is diametrically opposed to ours? Are they folks whose language or skin color is different from ours? We all have our prejudices, don't we? And though we don't like to admit it, deep down, we all have our hatreds, too. With most of the world consisting of unbelievers, it's quite likely that those we dislike or hate do not even know Jesus, and in many cases couldn't care less about Him. Are we content to let 'em all literally go to hell? That's pretty much the way Jonah felt until God got through his hard crust. What will it take for God to break through our hard-heartedness where the lost are concerned?

JONATHAN

And Jonathan had David reaffirm his oath out of love for him, because he loved him as he loved himself.

1 SAMUEL 20:17

Mention the name Jonathan and David's name immediately pops to mind, too. For theirs was the most powerful man-to-man friendship recorded in scripture. But life didn't always go smoothly for these friends. Though Jonathan was King Saul's eldest son, he could not control his father's actions against David. As the young commander who had killed Goliath for denigrating God became ever more popular, Saul became increasingly jealous—even to the point of madness.

Jonathan, a brave warrior who had single-handedly attacked the Philistines, felt such love for David that jealousy had no place in their relationship. Though he knew God was planning to replace Saul as king, Jonathan never became angry with David, who would take the throne. Being the heir to Saul's kingdom was less important than doing God's will. If God wanted his friend to rule, Jonathan would follow.

Their friendship began at first sight, and Jonathan made a covenant with his new friend. But their relationship was quickly strained as the people of Israel praised their new commander. Jealous Saul tried to kill David, first with his own hand, which held a spear, then by sending him into battle against the Philistines to earn the bride price for Saul's daughter Michal. When the Philistines didn't do the job for him, Saul tried to get Jonathan to kill David. Instead, the prince warned his friend and tried to convince Saul that David had only brought him good. For a while, the king seemed to agree, but again an evil spirit came on him and caused him to attack David. Michal helped her husband escape.

Jonathan kept in touch with his friend, much to his father's dissatisfaction. Saul began throwing spears at Jonathan, too. Knowing his father would kill David, Jonathan warned him with a prearranged sign.

Jonathan died in battle against the Philistines, along with his father and two of his brothers. David lamented their deaths but began a fight with Jonathan's brother Ish-bosheth for the throne God had promised him. After gaining the throne, David kept his covenant with Jonathan and treated Jonathan's son, Mephibosheth, kindly.

Jonathan's faithful character caused him to sacrifice much for his friend. Do we also look out for our friends' best interests, or are we too busy feeling jealous about their accomplishments?

JOSEPH OF ARIMATHEA

*Now when evening had come, there came a
rich man from Arimathea, named Joseph,
who himself had also become a disciple of Jesus.*

MATTHEW 27:57 NKJV

You're a high official within your country's governing body.
You have a reputation and wealth to safeguard, not to
mention the welfare of your own family. You've also been
secretly keeping company with a very controversial figure.
Being found out could mean your ruin. That's what Joseph
of Arimathea was up against when he walked into Pontius
Pilate's office to request the body of Jesus. Joseph did even
more than that, though. He and Nicodemus, a fellow
colleague from the Jewish Sanhedrin, took Jesus down
from the cross and laid Him to rest in a tomb that Joseph
owned. This took some courage. And because of the form
of execution, it also took a certain amount of "stomach."
Jesus' body was not a pretty sight at that point. This burial
was not for the faint of heart.

Joseph risked everything that day. He may very
well have been confronted by other colleagues who cast
aspersions on his deed. Some may also have had nothing
more to do with him from that day onward. Nonetheless,
by his daring that first Good Friday, Joseph personified the
word *nobility*.

What would we have done if we had been in his place?

JOSEPH, FOSTER FATHER OF JESUS

When [Joseph] arose, he took the young Child and
His mother by night and departed for Egypt.

MATTHEW 2:14 NKJV

Joseph had already been through trials that would have undone other, lesser men. He'd had to face the fact that his bride-to-be was already pregnant—and not by him! An angelic messenger told him to go ahead with his betrothal anyway, because Mary had conceived by the Holy Spirit. Then Joseph and his pregnant bride were forced to take an arduous journey to Bethlehem so he could register in the city of his ancestry for tax purposes. Upon arrival, they discovered that all the lodgings were sold out. Joseph and his wife had to camp out in a smelly stable. If that weren't enough, Mary went into labor and had her baby right then and there.

After the couple was visited by a strange retinue of wise men from the East, another angelic messenger told Joseph to make haste and flee—to Egypt! Talk about dedication. This man had it in spades. We never hear him grumble or complain. We don't hear much else about him beyond the flight to Egypt. Yet Joseph isn't merely a footnote in the New Testament. It was quiet, unassuming, obedient men like him whom God used masterfully to unfold His wondrous plan of salvation.

God is still filling His quiver with such men today.

JOSEPH, SON OF JACOB

*So Pharaoh said to Joseph, "I hereby put
you in charge of the whole land of Egypt."*

GENESIS 41:41

Joseph's birthday must have been one of the happiest days
in the lives of Jacob and his favorite wife, Rachel. But it
wasn't the happiest day in the lives of everyone in their
camp. For Jacob loved this son best of all, and his sons by
his other wives didn't appreciate it.

A typical youngster, when Joseph got an opportunity
to tattle on his older brothers, he took advantage of it. And
when he had dreams that showed he was more important
than they, he couldn't help but brag. So his siblings
retaliated when Dad was nowhere nearby. As his ten half
brothers watched over the family flocks, Joseph came by to
check up on them. The brothers tossed Dad's favorite in a
cistern for a while, then sold him into slavery when some
Midianite traders happened by. The ten took the many-
colored coat Jacob had given Joseph, dipped it in goat's
blood, and reported that Joseph was dead, killed by a wild
animal.

While Joseph discovered the hardships of slavery, Jacob
mourned the loss of his son. Joseph had been carried to
Egypt and sold into the household of Potiphar, Pharaoh's
captain of the guard. Despite his lack of freedom, Joseph
clung to his faith and served his new master well, for God
blessed him. That blessing drew the attention of Potiphar,

who promoted Joseph to take charge of his household. Although still a slave, Joseph was becoming upwardly mobile.

And even though Potiphar's wife lusted after Joseph, the faithful slave refused her repeatedly. Finally, she cornered Joseph and demanded that he sleep with her. Recognizing his dangerous situation, Joseph tore away from her, leaving his clothes in her hand.

Not to be disgraced, this unfaithful wife accused Joseph of attempting to seduce her. Enraged, Potiphar tossed Joseph into prison. But even there, Joseph prospered. He ended up in charge of all the prisoners. It wasn't the typical path to success, but Joseph was climbing the corporate ladder more quickly than he could know. It just didn't look like it at the moment.

After a while, two important prisoners were incarcerated: Pharaoh's cupbearer and baker. Joseph attended them. One night, each had a dream and wanted it interpreted, so Joseph obliged them. The cupbearer got good news: He would soon be released. But Joseph foresaw the death of the baker. And that's just what happened.

Though Joseph had asked the cupbearer to remember him, court life must have caught the fellow up. Not until two years later, when Pharaoh had a couple of bad dreams, did the cupbearer remember Joseph. Then the Hebrew slave was brought before Egypt's ruler. Joseph reported that the dreams Pharaoh had were dual warnings of a famine to come. He advised Pharaoh to plan ahead by gathering food in the good years that would precede lean ones. Immediately, Pharaoh appointed Joseph to oversee the project and set him over all Egypt. For seven years, he collected the country's grain.

Then the famine came, and people of all nations flocked to Egypt to buy grain. One day, Joseph's half brothers showed up. Untrusting, Joseph tested his siblings. He accused them of spying and held them in custody. After three days, he freed all but Simeon and required that they bring his younger brother, Benjamin, to him before he'd return Simeon to them.

Only when their food was very low would the brothers be able to convince Jacob to allow them to return to Egypt with Benjamin. In Egypt, Joseph again tested the ten, arranging to have Benjamin accused of stealing. But this time, instead of leaving their brother to slavery, the ten begged for his freedom.

Certain of his brothers' change of heart, Joseph revealed himself to them and arranged to bring the whole family into Egypt.

Joseph began as a thoughtless youth, but slavery and the dependence on God that it required brought him great wisdom that led to worldly success. When we suffer far less than slavery, do we use it as an opportunity to gain God's wisdom? What worked for Joseph will work for us, too.

Moses said to Joshua, "Choose some of our men and go out to fight the Amalekites. Tomorrow I will stand on top of the hill with the staff of God in my hands."

EXODUS 17:9

As Joshua led the Israelites in battle against the Amalekites, victory depended not on his battle plan, but on the hand of Moses. For when the prophet raised his hand, Israel prevailed. As the day wore on, some Israelite leaders held up weary Moses' hands, and Joshua led his people to victory. That battle, in which we first meet Joshua, shows us the hallmarks of his life: He became a strong fighting man of deep faith.

From youth, Joshua was Moses' right-hand man. Only Joshua accompanied Moses to Mount Sinai to receive the Ten Commandments. Moses' trusted assistant also spent much time in the Tent of Meeting, where the prophet spoke face-to-face with God. As the Israelites came to Canaan, Moses sent Joshua to spy out the new land. Of the twelve men on the mission, only Joshua and Caleb came back with a report based on faith instead of fear—and only those two men would come into the Promised Land when God allowed Israel to return to Canaan after their forty-year adventure in the desert.

As he neared death, Moses commissioned Joshua as his successor, and he must have known he had big shoes to fill. How humbling to know that he would complete the job

Moses had started: bringing the Israelites into their new land. Following Moses' death, God warned Joshua he'd need to be strong. He wasn't kidding. There was a lot of work ahead—and many battles. The job would demand all of Joshua's experience and faith.

Israel's first battle, at Jericho, was an amazing event. For six days, the warriors silently circumnavigated the city, accompanied only by the sound of the priests' ram's-horn trumpets. The people of Jericho must have found this God-designed attack pattern strange. On the seventh day, after they'd circled the city seven times, the Israelites let out a huge shout, and the walls of the city fell. Then Israel destroyed the metropolis, except for faithful Rahab, who had assisted the Israelite spies before the battle.

Israel as a whole had yet to learn a lesson that Joshua thoroughly understood: When they obeyed God, they would be successful, but when they sinned, they would fail. So they had to attack Ai twice in order to subdue it. When Joshua led them against the king of Jerusalem at Gibeon, the obedient warriors succeeded. God gave the king of Jerusalem and four other Amorite kings into the Israelites' hands. This was only the beginning of Joshua's lifelong conquest that still did not complete the task at hand.

God promised an aging Joshua that He would finish the conquest. He commanded Joshua to divide all the Promised Land between the tribes. After setting forth each tribe's property, Joshua shared God's promise of conquest with his people. Then he commanded them to obey God and His laws. "You shall cling to the LORD your God just as you have done to this day," he admonished them (Joshua 23:8 ESV). Otherwise, God would not drive out the nations from their land, and pagan nations would become a snare to Israel. Reminding them of God's covenant, Joshua called them to serve God alone and to put away foreign gods.

Joshua died at age 110 and was buried on his own land.

Have you heard that faith is for weaklings? Then look at Joshua, who combined deep trust in God with a strong warrior's arm. Given a challenging task, he spent his life accomplishing it. But even all the faith and experience at his command could not bring Israel's land under complete control. Ultimately, Joshua had to trust God for its completion.

Our lives may not be a continual battle, but we still relate to Joshua's war of faith. For we, too, rarely live in total peace. When God calls us to fight for Him, let's remind ourselves of faithful Joshua and look to our Lord for all the strength we need.

JOSIAH

*Josiah was eight years old when he became king,
and he reigned in Jerusalem thirty-one years. . . .
He did what was right in the eyes of the LORD.*

2 KINGS 22:1–2

Josiah followed two unusually wicked kings—his grandfather, Manasseh, and his father, Amon. These two did all they could to destroy the spiritual life of Judah. But at age sixteen, Josiah began to seek God, and four years later he began to eliminate the pagan influences in Judah by destroying idols and their altars.

In the eighteenth year of the good king's reign, when Josiah ordered repairs on the Temple, the high priest discovered Moses' Book of the Law. He immediately sent it to the king, who had it read to him. When Josiah discovered how far he and his people had strayed from God, he tore his robes in anguish.

He consulted the prophetess Huldah, who foresaw disaster but not during Josiah's life. Josiah had the book read to the people and reinstituted the celebration of Passover. But when Josiah went to battle against Pharaoh Neco, he was badly wounded by the Egyptian archers and died in Jerusalem.

We remember Josiah for his attitude about God's Word. He recognized its importance, made sure that people knew what it said, and encouraged others to obey its commands.

His attitude affected a nation.

Will we be known for loving and obeying the scriptures, or are we too busy obeying the call of something else?

JUDAS ISCARIOT

The evening meal was being served, and the devil had already prompted Judas Iscariot, son of Simon, to betray Jesus.

JOHN 13:2

Here's a man we love to hate. But he puzzles us, too, for Judas Iscariot walked daily with Jesus during His incarnation. Judas saw the miracles, heard the preaching, and had fellowship with Jesus and the other eleven disciples who were closest to Him. Yet this wayward disciple turned Jesus in to His enemies.

How could Judas do that? we wonder. He walked with Jesus, yet he led soldiers into the Master's presence. Judas had already offered Jesus up to the chief priests.

Did money get in the way of Judas's commitment to Jesus? After all, he was the keeper of the money donated to Jesus to provide for His little band of disciples. John records that Judas used to dip into the till for his own wants.

Perhaps money had its lure, but would that alone make Judas take this rash step? Probably not. It seems there would be more to gain from pilfering the disciples' purse than what he received from the priests for his betrayal.

In many ways, this disciple will always remain a mystery to us. Scripture doesn't divulge Judas's thoughts. Obviously he had some wrongheaded idea about who Jesus was and what He came to accomplish, but how did Satan tempt him? We may never know.

Judas brought the soldiers and Jewish officials to a private place where Jesus often met with the Twelve. He betrayed the Master with a kiss. What was he thinking? But the news that Jesus was condemned to death came as a surprise to him. What private world was Judas living in, to think the priests meant Jesus no harm?

When he discovered what he had done, after throwing the blood money into the Temple, Judas hanged himself in sorrow.

In a once-and-for-all act, Judas betrayed the Son, leading to the end of His earthly life. But while we question Judas's motives, are we aware that we aren't all that different from him? How easily we, too, fall into wrongheaded thinking and walk in ways that cannot glorify the Son. Despite the fact that we, too, have walked with Jesus, we easily fail.

Have we heard Jesus' call? Then let us remain vigilant so Satan's charms will not delude us. May our private worlds be centered on the Son, instead of on temptations that lead us astray.

KORAH

Korah son of Izhar, the son of Kohath, the son of Levi, and certain Reubenites—Dathan and Abiram, sons of Eliab, and On son of Peleth—became insolent and rose up against Moses. With them were 250 Israelite men, well-known community leaders who had been appointed members of the council.

NUMBERS 16:1–2

Moses and Aaron had a congregational rebellion on their hands. Factions within the worship community became jealous of Moses and his brother and tried to grab authority, accusing them of a misuse of power.

Kohath wanted to be a priest, even though his line of Levites had other duties in the Tabernacle. The Reubenites were angry because Moses had led them not into the Promised Land but into the desert again. Neither group asked God's opinion of their ideas.

Moses, far from intimidated, called on Korah and his followers to appear before God with their incense-filled censers at the ready. God would decide who was holy and who wasn't.

The next day, Korah gathered Moses' opponents among the Levites. But first the prophet went to the tents of the Reubenites, who had refused to appear at the Tent of Meeting. At their own tent doors, Moses confronted the rebels. There God split apart the earth beneath them, and it swallowed up their households and their men. Then fire came up and burned up the 250 men who were offering the incense.

Makes you think twice about starting a church rebellion, doesn't it?

LAZARUS

*Now a man named Lazarus was sick. He was from Bethany,
the village of Mary and her sister Martha. . . . So the sisters
sent word to Jesus, "Lord, the one you love is sick."*

JOHN 11:1, 3

When faithful Mary and Martha faced a crisis in their
brother's health, they knew where to turn. Sending a
message to Jesus, they requested Lazarus's healing. Then
the sisters waited, in nail-biting fear, for the Master to
appear. As the hours went on, they must have wondered
what had happened. Had their messenger failed them? Was
he hurt or killed? And as life receded, Lazarus might have
questioned whether Jesus could have betrayed him.

Jesus got the message, but He waited two days before
returning to Bethany to heal His friend. When He arrived,
mourning for Lazarus was in full force. The distraught
sisters were clearly puzzled that Jesus had not come sooner.
Lazarus had lain in the tomb for four days.

As Jesus commanded that the stone be rolled away, a
stunned Martha pointed out that the corpse by now would
be stinky. She had to wonder what Jesus was thinking.

Loudly, Jesus prayed to the Father and called Lazarus to
come out of the tomb. And his sisters, in amazement, saw
their sibling walk out of the grave, with linen still wrapped
around him and a cloth over his face. Suddenly, mourning
turned into delighted rejoicing—Lazarus had returned to
life.

The celebration didn't end there. People came from all over to hear of the man who'd returned from the grave. The report of this almost unbelievable event spread by a super-fast grapevine through the countryside. And many of the curious came to faith because of Lazarus's reporting skills.

When the chief priests heard of the event and the people's reaction, they plotted to kill both Jesus and Lazarus to hide the truth. They were successful with Jesus, but did Lazarus live? Scripture doesn't tell us how long Lazarus remained in this life after his resurrection. Was it years? We'll never know this side of heaven. But no matter if he lived weeks or years, his new life was a faith-filled success.

We know that Jesus still brings the dead back to life— many of us have closed the tomb door on sin and have experienced the joyous new life that only Jesus offers. And that's just a down payment on the future, when all believers will live eternally in Him.

[Abram] took. . .his nephew Lot, all the possessions they had accumulated and the people they had acquired in Haran, and they set out for the land of Canaan, and they arrived there.

GENESIS 12:5

Lot was raised by his grandfather Terah and then went to Canaan with his uncle Abram. But after a while their grazing land could not support both men's vast herds, so Abram let Lot choose where he wanted to live and moved his herd in another direction.

Lot chose the Jordan Valley and headed to a spot near Sodom. Perhaps this righteous man was somehow attracted by the sinful city. He eventually moved in and became a captive when the kings of Elam and Sodom fought. Abram had to rescue him.

Later, Lot offered hospitality to a couple of angels and tried to protect them from the wicked men of his city, who demanded sex with them. But Lot ended up being the rescued one, as the angels hustled him out of the soon-to-be-destroyed metropolis. On his way to safety, Lot saw his wife disobey the angels' command not to look back, and he saw her turned to salt.

The rest of the family sought shelter in a cave. His despairing daughters tricked Lot into incest so they would have children. Their sons became two of Israel's enemies.

Ever wonder what it's like to have one foot in the world and the other in God's kingdom? Then look at Lot.

Being somewhat worldly didn't bring him the benefits he expected. Instead, both Abram and God had to intervene to keep him from harm.

Does sin attract us? Beware! We, too, may need that rescuing angel.

LUKE

Our dear friend Luke, the doctor, and Demas send greetings.
COLOSSIANS 4:14

Luke was both a doctor and an excellent historian. But this well-educated man didn't spend time on his own public-relations campaign—he never even mentions himself as the author of the two biblical books that are credited to him: the Gospel that bears his name and the book of Acts.

Luke didn't meet Jesus personally. So when he wanted to describe Jesus' ministry, he did historical research. He left us with information that none of the other Gospel writers reported. Six miracles and nineteen parables appear only in his Gospel. We also read Mary's story of Jesus' birth and of the angels' visitation to the shepherds who witnessed His coming.

Luke's history has proven to be accurate. The map he draws of Paul's missionary journeys shows us the larger scope of life during the Roman Empire. The places and names are correct, and he appreciates differences in culture and language. In fact, this master of the word not only wrote excellent Greek, he properly reflected the use of other languages, too.

In Luke, we see a brilliant man totally dedicated to his mission for God. We know nothing of his job as a doctor, but as a Christian, he shines. Any believer would do well to walk in Dr. Luke's footsteps, no matter what the profession.

THE LUNATIC'S FATHER

Immediately the father of the child cried out and said with tears, "Lord, I believe; help my unbelief!"

MARK 9:24 NKJV

How many of us in our lives have spoken these words? Because of our fallenness, each of us is tied to this world. We are accustomed to harsh realities that so often seem overwhelming. They challenge our faith and make it difficult at times to believe God can help us.

This caring father was at his wit's end in seeking relief for his son, whom he watched being terribly afflicted by a demon. Imagine what it was like for him to repeatedly pull his child out of flames and out of water. We get the sense that his own sanity hung by a slender thread.

Then Jesus appears on the scene. He tells the father that if he can believe, all things are possible. The father, beside himself with desperation, probably screamed, "I do believe; help my unbelief!" For all his misfortune, here was an honest man. Jesus didn't take him to task for his lack of faith. Instead, He met the father and his son at their point of need and healed the boy right then and there.

No matter what our circumstances, Jesus is master of them all.

MALACHI

The oracle of the word of the LORD to Israel through Malachi.
MALACHI 1:1 NASB

The author of the last book of the Old Testament is a bit of an unknown quantity—we know very little indeed about him. Malachi was probably born in Judah and prophesied in Jerusalem. His book seems to have been written around 465 to 430 BC. Some scholars have even concluded that because his name means "my messenger," it was a title and not a proper name.

Ezra and Nehemiah would have been contemporaries of this minor prophet who spoke to the people in a time of adversity. Though they had returned to their homeland, the Israelites found life harder than they'd expected. God didn't appear to be helping them, so they started having serious doubts about Him. Their lives certainly proved their lack of faith, as they married into pagan families and ignored God's commands.

Though we don't have a lot of information about who Malachi was, it doesn't matter. The prophet had a revelation of God and His call to His people. Malachi called these hurting people back to obedience to their King and Creator.

Like Malachi, even if no one remembers the details of our lives, wouldn't we like others to benefit from our faithfulness? May God's message become our legacy to the future, even when our personal stories fade out.

MANASSEH

Manasseh was twelve years old when he began to reign, and he reigned fifty-five years in Jerusalem. And he did what was evil in the sight of the LORD.

2 CHRONICLES 33:1–2 ESV

Though his father, Hezekiah, was a good man, Manasseh turned in the opposite direction. Second Chronicles reports that Manasseh burned his sons as offerings to pagan gods, became involved in occult practices, and "did much evil in the sight of the LORD" (33:6 ESV). He even set up an idol in the Temple.

Manasseh led Judah to become worse than the Amorites, whom Israel had routed from Canaan. When Israel didn't respond to God's call to change, He got their attention another way. Assyria attacked Judah, captured their king, and dragged him to Babylon.

That got the king's attention! Manasseh called on God, who heard his pitiful cries, and the unfaithful king repented and returned to his throne. Manasseh removed the pagan altars from the city and restored the worship of the Lord. But he could not totally eradicate pagan practices in Israel.

Though Manasseh repented, he learned what many Christians have discovered: The influence of past sins doesn't entirely disappear. New believers must become witnesses to alter the influence that those past sins have on others' lives.

THE MAN BORN BLIND

As [Jesus] passed by, He saw a man blind from birth. And His disciples asked Him, "Rabbi, who sinned, this man or his parents, that he would be born blind?"

JOHN 9:1–2 NASB

In an age that knew very little science, Jews commonly believed that illness was caused by sin. Why would a good God inflict pain and suffering on one of His people?

The disciples were looking for a quick, easy answer that laid the blame on someone. If the parents had sinned, there was reason for God to have given them a blind child, and the disciples could go home happy. But why would God do this to an innocent child? Inquiring believers needed an answer.

Jesus made it clear that sin and illness do not necessarily equate. God had a purpose for this illness—it would bring glory to God as the Savior performed a healing.

While the disciples talked, the man must have waited hopefully. If he was not to blame, why shouldn't Jesus heal him? Hadn't He done such miracles before? Suddenly, Jesus' hand touched his eyes, spreading a combination of mud and saliva over them. Not the most pleasant way to be healed, but the man wasn't about to argue. At Jesus' direction, he rushed to wash in the pool of Siloam.

The blind man came back seeing. What delight to look on his neighbors' faces, to enjoy the world God had made, and to know that he would never again have to beg.

As he went, people started asking questions. Was this really the beggar, or just someone who looked like him? The man admitted the truth of his healing. But when he looked for Jesus, He was gone.

Instead, he came before the Pharisees, who were not pleased at this event and questioned him sternly about Jesus. Knowing no more, the man declared Him a prophet. So the unbelieving Pharisees questioned the man's parents. Fearful of being put out of the synagogue, they turned the issue back to their son's testimony. Again the rulers questioned the son, who did not budge. Did they want to become Jesus' disciples, he asked, since they were so interested?

So the rulers cast the man out of the synagogue. Then Jesus came to him. With answers to a few quick questions, the man understood and worshipped Him.

We have asked the disciples' questions when a child is hurt or ill or a devoted disciple is not healed. Can we accept that all will work out to God's glory, even if no earthly healing occurs? We may not have our answers on earth, but in heaven all will be clear.

MARK

Now Barnabas was determined to take with them John called Mark.

ACTS 15:37 NKJV

Whether he's called John, his Hebrew name, or Mark, his Greek name, this is the man who wrote the second Gospel, which reports the apostle Peter's outlook on Jesus' ministry.

Mark's mother was a believer who had a prayer meeting in her house. After Peter was freed from prison, he went there. The apostle seems to have been close to the family, because he refers to Mark as his son. Another of Mark's faithful family members, his cousin Barnabas, took Mark on a missionary journey with the apostle Paul. But at Perga, Mark left the missionary work, returning to Jerusalem. Paul didn't appreciate Mark's lack of stick-to-itiveness, and when a second missionary journey was in the offing, he refused Barnabas's suggestion that they give Mark another chance.

The disagreement became so fierce that it caused a rift between the two missionaries. Paul and Barnabas split up and spread the gospel separately. But by the end of his life, Paul had forgiven the errant missionary and let Mark again join him. The apostle even asked Timothy to bring Mark from Ephesus because he was "useful."

From useless to useful, Mark's life is a picture of a believer who grows in faith and consistency. He who draws near to God again, as Mark did, may become a valuable tool in the Lord's hand.

MATTHEW

As Jesus passed on from there, He saw a man named Matthew sitting at the tax office. And He said to him, "Follow Me." So he arose and followed Him.

MATTHEW 9:9 NKJV

One day, Jesus passed by a tax gatherer in Capernaum and called out, "Follow Me." And Levi, later called Matthew, dropped everything to dart after the Master.

Something powerful was at work with this man, who left behind wealth to spend his time on the road with Jesus. But Levi was delighted to make the change and threw a big feast for all his friends to introduce them to his new friend. To mark his new life, he even changed his name to Matthew, which means "a gift of God." The former tax collector must have felt this new life, with its spiritual freedom, had indeed been God's gift to him.

Later, Jesus selected Matthew as one of the Twelve—His closest disciples, who would go on to be apostles. Though scripture tells us no more of Matthew's mission, his Gospel speaks for itself. A book written in the last half of the first century, it reveals Jesus as Messiah to his fellow Jews.

Matthew depicts the joy of leaving sin behind to follow Jesus. No earthly wealth can bind us when we accept our Savior's love.

MELCHIZEDEK

Then Melchizedek king of Salem brought out bread and wine. He was priest of God Most High, and he blessed Abram, saying, "Blessed be Abram by God Most High, Creator of heaven and earth."

GENESIS 14:18–19

How little we know of this mystery man, who appears briefly in Genesis and receives more explanation in the New Testament than in the Old Testament.

Melchizedek emerged when Abram returned from rescuing Lot from the clutches of the king of Elam. This king of Salem (or "king of peace") came to Abram, carrying a banquet with him. He blessed Abram, using words that indicated he was speaking not of a Canaanite deity, but of the Lord God. And Abram responded by giving Melchizedek a tenth of the plunder he'd gained from the king of Elam and his allies.

If there was any question about whom this king-priest referred to, Hebrews 7 clears it up. The New Testament passage compares Salem's ruler with the Son of God—priest and king and superior to the Levite priesthood.

If nothing else, Melchizedek keeps us and our theology humble. We wonder just where this king came from and how he relates to Jesus. Is he Jesus, or just a picture of Him? Let's remember not to be too secure in our private interpretations. God doesn't tell us everything about Himself—or about mystery men like Melchizedek.

METHUSELAH

So all the days of Methuselah were nine hundred and sixty-nine years; and he died.

GENESIS 5:27 NKJV

You don't have to be a biblical scholar to have used the phrase "as old as Methuselah." He's become a byword for living an incredibly long life. He makes the centenarians of our age look positively youthful.

But Methuselah wasn't the only one in his family who did something unusual. His father, Enoch, "walked with God, and he was not, for God took him" (Genesis 5:24 ESV). First his father went to God without dying; then Methuselah lived such a long life that it probably seemed to his neighbors that he would never die. He finally passed on at the age of 969.

But scripture doesn't tell us any more about Methuselah's life. Was he a strong believer? Perhaps his faith contributed to his long life. But if he wasn't, perhaps the years dragged on seemingly unendingly.

How many years we live matters less than the way we live them. Are we endlessly seeking useless ways to fill idle hours? Or do we serve God with each moment? If we seek our Lord's will for each part of our day, whether we live a few years or many, we'll be blessed—and we'll be glad when we meet Jesus again.

MICAH

The word of the LORD that came to Micah of Moresheth during the reigns of Jotham, Ahaz and Hezekiah, kings of Judah—the vision he saw concerning Samaria and Jerusalem.

MICAH 1:1

Micah's name asked a question: "Who is like Yahweh?" But his name alone did not lead the people of Judah to understand God's greatness. Along with the prophet Isaiah, Micah confronted both Israel and Judah about their faithlessness. As we read the record of this minor prophet's preaching, we see that he didn't paint a pretty picture. More often than not, he spoke of judgment, though God's mercy and a promise of restoration also appear in his book.

Micah preached during the reigns of Jotham, Ahaz, and Hezekiah, kings of Judah during a difficult time. Assyria attacked and captured Israel, but God defended Judah when the Assyrian king Sennacherib attacked Jerusalem. Yet Jerusalem was not completely safe: Eventually, it would fall before Babylon, the pagan nation that replaced Assyrian power in the land.

Micah clearly prophesies the future Messiah and the peace that will flourish under His reign. Micah didn't speak the words his people wanted to hear, but he offered a hope that generations have treasured. The peace of the Messiah touches our lives, along with the hope of His eternal rule. How are we sharing that message with other hopeless hearts?

*Mordecai had a cousin named Hadassah, whom he had
brought up because she had neither father nor mother. This
girl, who was also known as Esther, was lovely in form and
features, and Mordecai had taken her as his own daughter
when her father and mother died.*

ESTHER 2:7

Kindhearted Mordecai took in his cousin when her parents
died, and he treated her like a daughter.

When Esther went, with many other beautiful young
women, to compete for the position of queen, Mordecai
may already have been a Persian official, because he already
lived in the citadel. No doubt his family had been part
of the Jewish nobility, exiled to Persia with the rest of the
Judean upper class.

When Esther went to the king, wise Mordecai had
warned her not to broadcast her Jewish heritage. Perhaps
because she did this, God used her to bring about the
salvation of His people.

After Esther became queen, Mordecai caught wind
of a plot to harm King Ahasuerus. The honest official
warned the queen, who passed word on to her husband.
The plotters were hanged and a record made of Mordecai's
actions. But before he could be rewarded, Mordecai got
into trouble with the wicked politician Haman.

The king had placed Haman in the highest political
position, but when everyone else bowed down to him

and paid homage, Mordecai refused. Scholars suggest that Haman, who is called an Agagite, supported King Agag, leader of the Amalekites and enemy of the Jews. In response, Haman overreacted and planned to kill both Mordecai and all his people. This powerful court official went to the king and bribed him to kill all the Jews in the Persian Empire. The king went along with the idea and had an edict written accordingly.

When Mordecai heard the news, he grieved publicly and reported the situation to Esther, even providing her with a copy of the edict. Esther doubted the wisdom of going to see the king. Unless he wanted to see her, she could be killed just for coming into his presence. Mordecai warned that cowardice would not save her, and who knew but that she had been put in her position "for such a time as this" (Esther 4:14)?

The queen went to her husband and was well received. She invited the king and Haman to two banquets. Before going to the second feast, Ahasuerus discovered that Mordecai had never been rewarded for foiling the plot against him. At Haman's suggestion, Esther's cousin was paraded through the streets and honored for his act. But when he discovered it was Mordecai who was to be so honored, not himself, the shock grieved Haman to his core.

At the second banquet, Esther revealed her own nationality and Haman's plot. Furious, Ahasuerus had Haman killed on the same gallows his henchman had prepared to kill Mordecai. Then the king requested that Mordecai draft a decree to protect the Jews from Haman's edict. According to Persian law, the king could not retract his original edict, but a new law allowed Jews to fight back against anyone who attacked them.

All Haman's lands became Mordecai's, and he was greatly honored by the king and raised to a high position. The Jews rejoiced, and on the day Haman had slated for their destruction, they destroyed all who came against them. The celebration of Purim was instituted to honor this day when God had protected His people.

Though God is not mentioned in the book of Esther, His presence is easy to see. He used the queen and her cousin to save His people from harm.

Mordecai courageously responded to God's call. Had he refused to act, or had Esther failed to confront the king, He would have found another way, but God often chooses to use His people to bring about great moments of salvation. It is a joy to those who obey and a blessing to those who receive the salvation. Will we be ready to respond if God calls us to do His will?

There the LORD showed him the whole land. . . .
"I have let you see it with your eyes, but you will not
cross over into it." And Moses the servant of the
LORD died there in Moab, as the LORD had said.

DEUTERONOMY 34:1, 4–5

As Moses stood looking at the Promised Land, he also
saw God's provision for His people. Because of their
disobedience, they had wandered for forty years in the
wilderness, but now the Israelites were headed into the
Promised Land flowing with milk and honey.

Moses knew what God's care meant in his life. Hadn't
the Lord watched over him when his mother placed him
in a basket and set him afloat on the Nile River? Without
God's intervention, would he have been picked up by a
softhearted Egyptian princess? Would he have grown up in
the court and learned how to deal with Pharaoh? God even
gave Moses his brother, Aaron, to speak for him and lead
the people's spiritual lives, and his sister, Miriam, to act as a
prophetess.

After killing a man in defense of his people, Moses
spent many years in the desert, herding sheep—perhaps a
great background for someone who would lead a stubborn
and rebellious people. For God called Moses to lead His
people from Egypt to the Promised Land of Canaan.

When the Israelites first heard of Moses' plan to lead
them to freedom, they were probably enthusiastic. But the

battle between Pharaoh and the prophet became long, dark, and dangerous as one plague after another hit the land. Still, God protected His people, gave them a celebration of the event in Passover, and led them to freedom.

As they set off, the trouble didn't stop. Egyptian warriors followed them and herded the slaves up against the Red Sea. Miraculously, God made a way for them to cross the sea and covered the pursuing army with water. Still, the people weren't satisfied. Before they walked through the sea, they were already complaining, "Why, Moses, did you take us out of our nice, cushy slavery? Are you going to let us die here?"

Dealing with periodic rebellion became part of Moses' job description, and he heard complaints about the food (or lack of food), the water, and every other part of the journey to their new land. Even when Moses went apart to receive God's Law, the irrepressible Israelites got into trouble, making a golden idol to worship. Yet neither God nor Moses gave up. God renewed His covenant with His people, and Moses led them on.

When God brought them to the Promised Land, the worst was yet to come. Moses sent twelve spies to check out the situation in Canaan. Ten came back saying, "We can never win over these people; they're too strong for us," as if they, not God, were in charge of the battle plan. Only two faithful men, Caleb and Joshua, encouraged the people to rely on God and take the land for themselves.

For forty years, the Israelites wandered around in circles, doing laps in the desert as punishment for their faithlessness. God provided manna to eat, laws to guide their spiritual lives, and much forgiveness. But until the original generation died, except for the two faithful spies, He would not lead them to the Promised Land again.

Not even Moses got to cross the border. He viewed it from afar, knowing God's promise would be fulfilled. But Moses died on Mount Nebo, just short of Canaan, and was buried in Moab.

The greatest prophet in Israel's history transmitted God's Law to the nation and took part in God's provision for His people, from salvation from Egypt to salvation of their souls. When pagan nations threatened, God protected them. When a harsh environment endangered them, God bestowed food and guided them in the right path.

Like Moses, do we, too, look back on our lives and see God's provision? When we see His great works, are we thankful, or do we simply seek another benefit? Let's appreciate all God has done for us, unlike those faithless Israelites who perished in the desert.

NAAMAN

So Naaman said, ". . . Yet in this thing may the
LORD pardon your servant: when my master goes into
the temple of Rimmon to worship there, and he leans on my
hand, and I bow down in the temple of Rimmon—when
I bow down in the temple of Rimmon, may the LORD
please pardon your servant in this thing."

2 KINGS 5:17–18 NKJV

Naaman was an able and valiant military commander for
the king of Syria. He was also a leper. In ancient times,
leprosy was an incurable, dread disease that disfigured the
body.

Happily for Naaman, a young Israelite woman captured
by Syrian raiders was serving in his home. This young
woman believed the prophet Elisha could cure Naaman and
said as much to her mistress. When Naaman was told, he
went off to see Elisha.

When Naaman arrived at Elisha's house, the prophet
sent out a servant to tell him to bathe in the Jordan seven
times. This wasn't good enough for Naaman, who was
expecting much more. Leaving in a purple rage, he finally
relented, when persuaded by his aides, and heeded the
prophet's counsel. Dunking seven times in the Jordan, he
was cured of his leprosy. Overwhelmed by his cure, Naaman
vowed to worship no god but the God of Israel.

Then we're told that Naaman asked for pardon
whenever he would accompany his master into the pagan

house of Rimmon and bow with him. At first, this request appears to cast doubt on the genuineness of Naaman's conversion. Instead of lowering the boom on him, Elisha told him to go in peace. Elisha trusted God to work out the matter in Naaman's heart.

If we commit to walk with God, we cannot hold on to any sin. Only God can enable us to make that kind of commitment, as He likely did for Naaman.

NATHAN

Then the LORD sent Nathan to David. And he came to him, and said to him: "There were two men in one city, one rich and the other poor."

2 SAMUEL 12:1 NKJV

The prophet Nathan is best known as a storyteller who came to King David with a tale that made the ruler understand his sin.

This wasn't the first time Nathan had brought David bad news. The godly king had wanted to build a temple for the Lord. Recognizing David's spiritual fervor, Nathan directed him to start. But God told the prophet to halt the building plans, for they were not His plan. Humble David accepted Nathan's redirection.

Maybe that gave Nathan the courage to confront David after the king had taken Bathsheba for himself, despite the rights of her husband, Uriah. David, the rich man in Nathan's story, took advantage of poor Uriah, who had only one lamb. When David recognized the point of story, he repented of his sin in setting Uriah up to be killed and taking Bathsheba for himself.

No bad feelings destroyed the relationship between prophet and king. At the end of David's life, Nathan worked to warn the king that another son was deposing the heir, Solomon.

Nathan was a brave man who followed God's directions. Though offending the king would have been dangerous, the prophet cared more for God than for man—even a very powerful man.

Do we?

NATHANAEL

Jesus saw Nathanael coming toward Him, and said of him,
"Behold, an Israelite indeed, in whom is no deceit!"

JOHN 1:47 NKJV

Nathanael is a bit player in scripture who stands out in
our minds. His story appears in a single paragraph, but we
don't forget him.

This forthright man, approached by Philip with the
news that Jesus was Messiah, didn't immediately pray
the sinner's prayer. But Jesus did not condemn him for
responding, "Can anything good come out of Nazareth?"
(John 1:46 NKJV). On meeting this less-than-tactful man,
Jesus declared him to be without deceit. Nathanael still had
questions for Jesus. But the news that He'd seen him under
the fig tree was proof enough. This plain-spoken man
called Him Messiah.

Jesus promised that Nathanael would see much more
than this simple miracle. Jesus told him that he would see
heaven open.

Like Nathanael, who is also called Bartholomew in
the lists of the Twelve, we need to study the scriptures.
Nowhere had the Old Testament referred to the Messiah as
coming from Nazareth. So Nathanael had honest doubts.
He came to Jesus seeking to know the truth.

Are we honest seekers, or do we come to God with an
agenda? How will our Bible study be different if we only
seek to discover the truth God has for us today?

In the second year of the reign of Nebuchadnezzar,
Nebuchadnezzar had dreams; his spirit was troubled,
and his sleep left him.

DANIEL 2:1 ESV

Nebuchadnezzar, king of Babylon, ruled the most powerful nation in the world. But conquering the world didn't solve his problems, though he commanded an army that brought fear into the hearts of its enemies. So the king became a very angry person.

In 605 BC, Nebuchadnezzar conquered Judah and took the finest young men of that nation back to Babylon. Among them were Daniel and his companions, Shadrach, Meshach, and Abednego, who proved themselves wise beyond the king's expectation, better than all his pagan magicians.

One night when the king had counted hundreds of sheep but still couldn't sleep because of his bad dreams, he commanded his magicians to tell him what was wrong.

"Tell us your dream," the men requested. But the king, tired of lies and prevarication, adamantly refused. They must tell him the dream and its interpretation or he would kill them.

"No one," the magicians insisted, "can do that. Only the gods can interpret this dream." So the king prepared to carry out his threat.

When the captain of the guard sought to kill him,

Daniel insisted on making an appointment with the king. Before they met, God gave Daniel a vision concerning the king's dream. When Daniel revealed the nightmare and its meaning, Nebuchadnezzar worshipped the Lord, and the magicians were spared.

However, this power-hungry king hadn't gained humility or true faith. Nebuchadnezzar set up an idol and expected everyone to worship him. So Daniel's three friends spent time in a fiery furnace and were saved only by God. Again the king worshipped the Lord, but again he didn't quite understand.

Finally, Nebuchadnezzar had a bad dream of a tall, beautiful tree that was lopped down to a stump. When the king's magicians couldn't interpret the dream, Daniel told the king it meant his own humiliation until he accepted God's authority. A year later, as the king boasted of his own power, Daniel's prophecy came true. Nebuchadnezzar was driven out from mankind and chomped on grass, like an ox, living in the wild. When the fallen king recognized God's power, he received his reason back and praised the Lord.

Spiritually empty, Nebuchadnezzar tried to fill the vacuum with his own greatness. This useless spiritual tactic never worked for him, and it won't work for us, either. Only God can fill the immense vacuum in our hearts that is just His size.

*The words of Nehemiah son of Hacaliah: In the month of
Kislev. . .Hanani, one of my brothers, came from Judah with
some other men, and I questioned them about the Jewish
remnant that survived the exile, and also about Jerusalem.*

NEHEMIAH 1:1–2

Though Nehemiah held a prestigious position in the
Babylonian court, he wasn't happy. As long as his people in
Jerusalem lived in danger, this exiled Jew's heart remained
with them. Hanani had reported that Jerusalem's walls were
broken and the gates destroyed, and Nehemiah knew that
meant invaders could easily destroy what was left of Judah's
capital city. Nehemiah immediately mourned, wept, and
prayed.

While Nehemiah waited on King Artaxerxes I, his
sorrow became apparent. Powerful kings weren't used to
their cupbearers looking as if they were about to dilute the
wine with tears. But when Artaxerxes heard of Nehemiah's
problem, he supported his desire to help Judah. In a few
minutes, Nehemiah had permission to go to his homeland,
provision for his journey, and authorization to get building
materials.

Three days after he arrived in Jerusalem, Nehemiah
quietly made a nighttime inspection of the walls he'd heard
so much about. Then he informed the city officials that
they needed to rebuild. What could they say but yes?

Meanwhile, other voices screamed, "No!" The leaders

of the surrounding nations liked having Judah weak and helpless. So local leaders of neighboring lands, Sanballat, Tobiah, and Geshem, accused Nehemiah of rebellion. The city building project began with guards surrounding Jerusalem and prayers being lifted up for God's protection. Even the workers wore swords.

Once the wall and gates were rebuilt, Governor Nehemiah reformed Jerusalem's politics and brought his people back to faith. But when he left to report to Artaxerxes and came back to discover that the job was far from completed, he faithfully continued the necessary work.

When we're taking on a project for God, do we expect all the wheels to run smoothly, the gas to be cheap, and our fellow travelers to support us? It doesn't always work that way. Nehemiah had opposition from within his own people and from outsiders. When he wanted to build, he had to hand his laborers swords. Resistance sometimes indicates we're doing just what God wants—and what Satan detests. So let's work faithfully, even when unbelievers argue. We're working for God, not the enemy!

NICODEMUS

Nicodemus answered and said to Him,
"How can these things be?"

John 3:9 nkjv

The Sanhedrin was Israel's supreme council and court of justice in the first century. Its members, leading figures and more often than not men of means, had reputations to consider. Perhaps that's why one of them, Nicodemus, came to Jesus by night. By now, Jesus' fame had spread far and wide throughout Israel. Many regarded Him as a great prophet "mighty in deed and word" (Luke 24:19 nkjv). But the Jewish leaders didn't exactly approve of this new prophet.

Nicodemus had obviously thought a lot about Jesus, as evidenced by his words: "Rabbi, we know that You are a teacher come from God; for no one can do these signs that You do unless God is with him" (John 3:2 nkjv). Nicodemus took Jesus seriously.

Yet Jesus responded jarringly. "Most assuredly, I say to you, unless one is born again, he cannot see the kingdom of God" (John 3:3 nkjv). To Nicodemus, it must have seemed a strange and incredible statement. You can imagine his face contorting in puzzlement as he began struggling to comprehend what he had just heard. "Stay with me Nicodemus; there's more," you can almost hear Jesus respond. But He continued, "Most assuredly, I say to you, unless one is born of water and the Spirit, he cannot enter the kingdom of God. That which is born of the flesh is flesh, and that which is born of the Spirit is spirit. Do not marvel that I said to you, 'You must be born again.' The wind blows where it wishes, and you hear the sound of it, but cannot tell where it comes from and where it goes. So is everyone who is born of the Spirit" (John 3:5–8 NKJV). Nicodemus, by now totally befuddled, replied, "How can these things be?"

With that question and Jesus' subsequent answer, Nicodemus was brought to a heavenly plane of understanding. The evidence of his comprehension? Nicodemus stood up in defense of Jesus (see John 7:50–52) and joined Joseph of Arimathea in burying Jesus' body (see John 19:39), two actions fraught with risk for a Jewish leader.

We can fault Nicodemus for using the cover of darkness to meet with Jesus, but darkness or not, he met with Jesus. Furthermore, he was serious about his inquiries into Jesus' teaching, though at first he couldn't quite grasp what Jesus told him. How seriously do we take Jesus? Is He nothing more than a distant figure of history, or is He as alive to us as anyone living can be? Only the Holy Spirit, blowing on the embers in our hearts, can fan them into the same flame of conviction that Nicodemus had.

NOAH

Thus Noah did; according to all
that God commanded him, so he did.

GENESIS 6:22 NKJV

Cataclysm: Webster's defines this word as "a momentous and violent event marked by overwhelming upheaval and demolition." In our all-too-distracted lives, do we have any idea the number of cataclysms God has spared us from on this planet? Should a tenuous section of one of the Canary Islands give way and fall into the Atlantic, it would generate a monstrous tidal wave that would destroy the entire East Coast of the United States as well as many other parts of the Atlantic. For those who live on the Indian Ocean, the prospect of a tsunami became a terrifying reality on December 26, 2004. For all our technology, we are still vulnerable!

Not long after God created humankind, His forbearance ran out, and He decided to bring a cataclysm upon the earth. He selected a man named Noah to undertake the world's first shipbuilding project, but not until after He told Noah what He planned to do.

Noah was a descendant of Seth, Adam and Eve's third child. The children in this line sought God faithfully at first. One of them was a man by the name of Enoch, whom God translated alive into heaven body and soul. Noah was Enoch's great-grandson. The descendants of Cain, on the other hand, were unfaithful to God and thus became corrupt. In time, the corruption of Cain's descendants had spread so malevolently as to also contaminate Seth's line. The cancer of sin spread virulently on the earth and became deeply ingrained in humans. In short, in the eyes of God, humanity was too far gone.

What an awful time it was to be alive back then. Society (if you could call it that) ran wild with every kind of crime and vice imaginable, and did so with impunity! It was a world not fit for man or beast. It was in such a world that Noah lived.

Aside from his building of the ark, scripture doesn't tell us much else about Noah. Still, we wonder how any man or woman could have survived spiritually in such a society. We can only imagine the kind of pressures Noah faced, the allurements and enticements of a world that had become hell on earth. Apart from God's saving grace, could any human have survived? Only by God's grace was blameless Noah able to resist the downward pull of all the evil surrounding him and rise above it.

Undoubtedly, he had to contend with heaps of ridicule toward his God-given nautical project. Perhaps the area in which he lived was far from any sizable body of water. That would have made his project all the more ludicrous. Still, in unquestioning obedience, Noah kept building. It is also quite likely that he became an evangelist—perhaps the first one since the Creation! Knowing what was to befall those he knew must have propelled him to sound a clarion alarm, whether or not anyone would listen. Surely those who mocked ceased their mocking and paused in wonder when they witnessed a vast, orderly train of animals streaming toward the ark, all led by an invisible hand.

Then came the day when God ushered Noah and his family aboard and sealed them within the ark. It was all over but the waiting. The ridicule reached a crescendo. Can you imagine the jeering and taunts and laughter of those outside? Seven days later, the laughter changed to cries of horror. In a moment, relatives, neighbors, friends, and acquaintances were all swept away by the deluge. There was nothing Noah or his family could do about it. What a fearful death! Only Noah and his family were spared. And with this event, the world got a picture of God's salvation. A piece of the world floated safely atop the oceans until He brought them onto dry land again.

Noah went against a mighty tide of sin. Until spared, he paid a dear price for it, and so must we as ambassadors and apologists for Jesus. Like Noah, our faithfulness to God's Word will be contrary to everything the world stands for. But every time we see a rainbow, it reminds us of His faithfulness!

PAUL

*Continue in your faith, established and firm, not moved from
the hope held out in the gospel. This is the gospel that you
heard and that has been proclaimed to every creature under
heaven, and of which I, Paul, have become a servant.*

COLOSSIANS 1:23

A zealous Jew and a Pharisee, well educated as a pupil of
Gamaliel, Saul of Tarsus probably could have quoted the
Old Testament better than many Christians of his day. But
until Jesus laid him flat on the road to Damascus, religion
was a matter of rules and regulations to Saul. Getting
knocked down and blinded during his road trip got this
Pharisee's attention. Understanding how spiritually sightless
he'd been, he accepted Jesus as Messiah.

As soon as he started preaching his newfound faith,
persecution became Saul's lot. He had to escape from
Damascus to avoid death. For the next three years, he lived
in Arabia.

Returning to Jerusalem, Saul faced a new kind of
persecution. Christian leaders doubted his conversion.
Was this some new ploy to infiltrate their community? But
Barnabas supported Saul. Finally, the former persecutor
of Christians was accepted into the church and began
preaching.

The Holy Spirit chose Barnabas and Saul for a
missionary journey, and they sailed for Cyprus. Scripture
first records that here Saul was called by his Roman name,

Paul. The missionaries started preaching to the Jews, but opposition in the synagogues grew. At Lystra, Paul was stoned by Jews from Antioch and Iconium and left for dead. Clearly Paul's real mission would be to the Gentiles. Before long, Christians began asking, "Should new converts have to follow Jewish practices like circumcision?" Paul and Barnabas debated the issue in Antioch, then went to Jerusalem, where the council of leaders agreed that Gentile circumcision was unnecessary.

After the two missionaries reported back to Antioch, Barnabas wanted to return to the new churches they'd founded. But he and Paul seriously disagreed about whether to take Barnabas's cousin John Mark with them. John Mark had dropped out of their previous mission, and now Paul didn't want him along. So the companions split up, and each took another man along to begin a fresh mission.

Paul's new road was not an easy one. He got more beatings than kudos, and even the believers he spoke to often gave him grief. Paul continued the plan he and Barnabas had begun, going into a town, preaching to those who would listen, and establishing a church of converts. When Paul was traveling, he wrote letters addressing the most crucial issues in the churches he'd founded. These became the biblical epistles to the churches of Greece, Rome, and Asia Minor. Periodically, Paul returned to these young churches to encourage them in their faith and to address doctrinal issues.

As he went, Paul also developed new leaders, taking men like Titus and Timothy along to learn the ropes. Then they, too, trained the people in the growing congregations.

Eventually, the turmoil that followed the apostle's message caught up with him in Jerusalem, where a group of Jews accused him of wrong teaching and defilement of the Temple. Though the charges were spurious, Paul ended up appealing to Roman law and being sent to Rome. He lost his life as a martyr in Emperor Nero's persecutions.

Paul was a highly dedicated Christian, a servant of Christ. Whether he was being threatened by a shipwreck on his way to Rome or standing before a cantankerous ruler, he stood firm for Jesus. So it's not surprising that Paul's epistles describe a brass-tacks religion. There's a lot of practical help here for struggling new Christians or mature believers who need to address a problem in their congregations or personal lives. Paul recognized that faith is a matter of what you do, as well as what you think and believe.

Are we inspired by Paul's demanding view of faith? Or do we discount it as something no modern-day believer could accomplish? On our own, we could never reach the world for Jesus. But empowered by His Spirit, we feel inspiration, not confrontation, as we look at the life of His servant Paul.

*When Simon Peter saw it, he fell down at Jesus' knees, saying,
"Depart from me, for I am a sinful man, O Lord!"*

LUKE 5:8 NKJV

He might seem the least likely man to become an apostle
of Jesus. Rough-hewn, hard working, and relatively
uneducated, Simon, son of Jonah, was a no-nonsense kind
of man. He may have been a bit coarse and vulgar, too. As
a fisherman, he had his good business days and not-so-good
days.

Simon was in a business partnership with Zebedee,
father of James and John, whom Jesus would also call
to apostleship. Jesus had referred to them as "Sons of
Thunder," perhaps implying their father had a fiery temper.
Were that so, it's possible that Simon and Zebedee had their
quarrels, some of which were probably high volume/low
prosperity.

Then came the day that Simon's younger brother
Andrew told him that he'd met the long-awaited Messiah.
We have to wonder what Simon thought about his brother's
news and how he reacted when he first met Jesus. Top that
with Jesus' immediately giving Simon the name Peter (or
"Rock").

Next, a momentous event occurred. After using Peter's
fishing boat as a waterborne pulpit, Jesus tells Peter to put
out from the shore and cast his net over the side for a catch.
Having had one of his not-so-good days, Peter is reluctant

at first but then agrees to Jesus' request. In no time Peter hauls in perhaps his greatest catch ever. Sensing something supernatural is taking place, Peter falls at Jesus' knees, begging Him, "Depart from me, for I am a sinful man, O Lord!" (Luke 5:8 NKJV).

We wonder what made Peter say what he did, but more important, what was it about Jesus that made him say it? Clearly, Peter didn't let his sinfulness keep him from following Jesus to become a fisher of men.

Another momentous event occurred in the synagogue at Capernaum. Jesus said, "Whoever eats My flesh and drinks My blood has eternal life, and I will raise him up at the last day. For My flesh is food indeed, and My blood is drink indeed" (John 6:54–55 NKJV). Nothing like this had been heard before in any synagogue. Those listening recoiled in horror. People muttered, "How can this Man give us His flesh to eat?" (John 6:52 NKJV). Sadly, many chose to leave Jesus right then and there.

Jesus turned to His apostles and asked if they wanted to leave, too. Peter replied at once, "To whom shall go?" and then added, "You have the words of eternal life. Also we have come to believe and know that You are the Christ, the Son of the living God" (John 6:68–69 NKJV). Peter had an understanding of who Jesus was, though it was far from complete.

Finally, on the night before Jesus' death, He gathered with His disciples for His last Passover meal. During the meal, Jesus foretold how all of the disciples would abandon Him later that evening. As always, stalwart Peter proclaimed that he would never leave Jesus, even if everyone else did. If he had to die with Jesus, he would not deny him (see Matthew 26:31–35).

Jesus replied, "Will you lay down your life for My sake? Most assuredly, I say to you, the rooster shall not crow till you have denied Me three times" (John 13:38 NKJV). If that came close to breaking Peter's heart, what Jesus said next probably made it skip a beat. "Simon, Simon! Indeed, Satan has asked for you, that he may sift you as wheat. But I have prayed for you, that your faith should not fail; and when you have returned to Me, strengthen your brethren" (Luke 22:31–32 NKJV). The prospect was both chilling and encouraging. Oh yes, Satan would sift, and sift he did, but Jesus would triumph in the life of Peter.

Peter went from an impulsive, headstrong follower to a Spirit-filled leader. God took a raw lump of coal and refined it for His purposes. He will do the same with each of us if we put aside our own pride and ego.

PHARAOH

"When Pharaoh does not listen to you, then I will lay My hand on Egypt and bring out My hosts, My people the sons of Israel, from the land of Egypt by great judgments."

EXODUS 7:4 NASB

The ancient Egyptians believed that their pharaoh was a god; and if anyone let that idea go to his head, it was the pharaoh who ruled during the age of Moses.

Though we know all about his authority and the events recorded in scripture, one thing we don't know is this ruler's name. The Bible calls him simply "Pharaoh," yet because the history of that era is so vague, we don't know for certain which Egyptian pharaoh went head-to-head with God and His prophet Moses.

What we do know is that this was a major contention. Moses and his brother, Aaron, confronted Pharaoh, asking him to free the enslaved Hebrews. As God had forewarned Moses, Pharaoh would have none of it. When Aaron threw down his rod and it turned into a snake, the Egyptian magicians did the same, only to have their snakes eaten by Aaron's.

When Pharaoh did not heed Moses' request, God, who had hardened the Egyptian ruler's heart, gave Pharaoh ten attention-getting plagues: turning water to blood; overrunning the land with frogs; covering the earth with gnats; filling Egyptian homes and ruining the land with flies; killing livestock; afflicting man and beast with boils;

killing animals, plants, and people with hail; destroying with locusts what few crops were left; and covering the entire land with darkness. When none of these plagues worked, God finally took the life of the firstborn of every Egyptian animal and human.

Pharaoh might have gotten high marks for stubbornness, but his attitude ruined his country before he thrust the Hebrews out of Egypt. Yet even then he made an unwise decision and sent his army in pursuit of the former slaves in an attempt to return them to his kingdom, but it was too late. As God's people miraculously crossed the Red Sea, the Egyptian army followed and was destroyed in the waters.

Stubbornness has its uses, but only when combined with godly wisdom. Pharaoh ran aground when he defied God and was willing to go to any lengths to get his own way. Will we learn from him before we, too, head down our own path, ignoring the call of God?

PHILEMON

Paul, a prisoner of Christ Jesus, and Timothy our brother, to Philemon our beloved friend and fellow laborer.

PHILEMON 1:1 NKJV

Faithful Philemon must have felt honored to receive a personal message from the apostle Paul. But the topic of Paul's note wasn't such a pleasant one, and perhaps Philemon would have preferred not to share its contents with his house church. Philemon's slave Onesimus had run away from his master, and Paul expected the wealthy slave owner to be justly angry when he discovered that Onesimus was with Paul in Rome.

Yet Onesimus had become a Christian under Paul's ministry. And for Paul, the once-useless slave now lived up to the meaning of his name: "useful." The apostle would rather have kept Onesimus with him, but he sent the slave back with a request that Philemon treat him as a brother in Christ. Some scholars think the apostle might even have been encouraging Philemon to free him and return him to Paul.

Philemon had a hard time viewing slaves as people, but Paul impressed upon him the need to do so. Are there some "less important" or less-than-lovable people in our lives? God calls us to be gentle Philemons, especially toward our brothers in Christ. They're no less important to God than this first-century slave was.

PHILIP THE APOSTLE

The next day Jesus decided to leave for Galilee.
Finding Philip, he said to him, "Follow me." Philip, like
Andrew and Peter, was from the town of Bethsaida.

JOHN 1:43–44

With His usual brief "Follow Me," Jesus called Peter's fellow townsman to discipleship. And the newly commissioned Philip didn't sit on the good news. The next day, he shared it with Nathanael: "We have found the one Moses wrote about in the Law" (John 1:45). When Nathanael doubted, Philip didn't argue; he just invited his friend to check out Jesus.

Again we see Philip at the feeding of the five thousand, when Jesus asks him, "Where can we buy bread to feed these people?" (John 6:5 THE MESSAGE). Philip recognizes the problem but cannot solve it.

Philip's real skill was leading people to Jesus, as he did with some Greeks who asked to see Him. When Jesus began getting into deep theology, at the end of His ministry, Philip, confused, asked to see the Father. He may not have been a heavyweight theologian, but Philip still had an important mission—bringing others to Jesus. Whereas some might have felt intimidated, he became excited. It didn't matter whether he had all the answers; this disciple just wanted people to know his friend and Savior.

Do we share Philip's zeal for making Jesus known?

PHILIP THE EVANGELIST

*Then Philip went down to the city of
Samaria and preached Christ to them.*

ACTS 8:5 NKJV

One of seven deacons chosen for their good reputations
and willingness to serve, Philip was part of the first
church growth experience. Even as Saul's persecution of
Christianity grew, the number of believers expanded.

Because they were tossed out of Jerusalem, Christians
started preaching wherever they went. In Samaria, Philip
had so much evangelistic success that Peter and John were
sent to expand the mission. Receiving word from an angel,
Philip headed on toward Gaza. In the desert, he ran into an
Ethiopian eunuch who was reading from the book of Isaiah.

"Do you understand what you're reading?" Philip asked
the man, who invited the evangelist to explain it to him.
What a wonderful opportunity to preach Jesus to a wide-
open heart. As soon as they found water, the eunuch asked to
be baptized. Philip completed the rite and then was carried
away by the Spirit, leaving a praise-filled eunuch behind him.

The last time scripture mentions Philip, Paul stops
by his home in Caesarea. Philip not only reached others
with the gospel, but his family believed, too. He had four
believing daughters who prophesied.

Wherever he went, Philip brought along his message.
Do we do the same? Or do we only talk about Jesus when
we're at church?

PONTIUS PILATE

*"What shall I do, then, with Jesus
who is called Christ?" Pilate asked.*

MATTHEW 27:22

These words, thundering down to us through the corridors
of time, were spoken by a man caught up in the pomp and
circumstance of his own office as governor of a troublesome
outlying Roman province. Here we have a striking
confrontation between the quintessential autocrat and God
incarnate!

Pontius Pilate was what we would call a "company
man." He knew (or thought he knew) which side his bread
was buttered on. His allegiance was to Rome, not to the
ideology of an occupied people. No doubt he knew of their
heritage, including the God whom they worshipped and to
whom their Temple was dedicated. While all of this might
have made him wonder, there can also be no doubt that he
valued Roman power and prestige over the religion of Israel.
Perhaps he thought, *If their God is so great, how did He
allow them to fall under our heel of iron?*

Then he met their Messiah face-to-face. At Passover, a
boisterous crowd gathered outside the Praetorium, Pilate's
headquarters in Jerusalem. The mob, replete with the Jewish
leaders of the day, brought a man with them. He stood out
from the rest of the crowd, His bearing noble yet besieged.
They accused him with trumped-up charges, such as
"perverting the nation, and forbidding [people] to pay taxes

to Caesar" (Luke 23:2 NKJV), a charge obviously designed to get Pilate's attention.

As Pilate sized up the accused, he must have sensed that no ordinary man stood before him. This is evident by the train of interaction that follows between Pilate and Jesus and the crowd. Pilate seemingly did not suffer trifles lightly. "You take Him and judge Him according to your law" (John 18:31 NKJV), said the governor to the crowd. "Don't bother me with petty crimes you are capable of handling," was the implication.

But the crowd was not so easily dismissed. Before long, Pilate realized that the people were clamoring for nothing less than Jesus' blood. Then began an interrogation by Pilate to assess Jesus' guilt, one that would lead Pilate to understand what was really going on. Scripture says, "For he knew that they had handed Him over because of envy" (Matthew 27:18 NKJV). Pilate, who had the power either to release Jesus or to crucify him (see John 19:10), found himself trying to save a man who otherwise would have meant nothing to him. What prompted Pilate to act this way? Was it Jesus' admission that He was a king and that His kingdom was not of this world? Was it the crowd's accusation that Jesus had declared Himself to be the very Son of God? Was it his wife's urging to "have nothing to do with that just Man" (Matthew 27:19 NKJV)?

In any event, the mob finally cried out, "If you release this Man, you are no friend of Caesar; everyone who makes himself out to be a king opposes Caesar" (John 19:12 NASB). Here were words that Pilate clearly understood, and they must have rattled him. Things were beginning to get out of hand, and Pilate, ever the shrewd administrator, sensed the situation was only a few steps away from becoming a full-fledged riot. Not exactly the stuff a Roman governor wanted to be known for—and certainly not with these people who were already fed up with Roman domination.

If Pilate was a risk taker, he was at his limit. Like Julius Caesar before him, he had arrived at the banks of his own Rubicon—without even realizing it. Would he refrain, or would he cross? Tragically, Pilate swallowed the mob's raging words and "surrendered Jesus to their will" (Luke 23:25).

Where do we stand when the going gets rough, when our allegiance to Jesus is tested? Since that fateful day in Jerusalem, many martyrs throughout the centuries have answered Pilate's question with their own lives. Most of us will never face execution. But scorn, ridicule, and perhaps even persecution will come. Then we will not be able to avoid the question, "What shall I do, then, with Jesus who is called Christ?" (Matthew 27:22).

THE PRODIGAL SON

Jesus continued: "There was a man who had two sons. The younger one said to his father, 'Father, give me my share of the estate.' So he divided his property between them."

LUKE 15:11–12

This character in one of Jesus' parables may not have been a real person, but he's very true to life. You probably know someone like him—or maybe your life before you met Jesus was not unlike this young man's.

As the prodigal son grabbed his inheritance, packed his bags, and set out to see the world, life looked good. Like many young men, he wanted to test his ability to do what he pleased. High living appealed to him, and when he got to a foreign land, he quickly engaged in just about every sin available.

But money spent on loose living is a bad investment. In time, the prodigal found himself penniless. The moment he clinked his last two coins together, all his so-called friends disappeared. Now that he couldn't buy the wine, women, and song, the prodigal wasn't worth their time.

As life often has it, just as the money disappeared, a severe famine arose. Now the boy had two troubles. How would he feed himself? No one was looking to hire an experienced wastrel. Maybe his reputation went before him, because the boy ended up tending pigs. Caring for an unclean animal would have been abhorrent to a good Jew. The lad was as low as he could go, both spiritually and physically.

Just as this vagabond was contemplating how good pig pods would taste, an idea struck him: *My father's servants eat better than this!* So he planned to return to his father, not as a favored son, but as an abject servant. After composing a nice, humble speech designed to persuade his father to let him become a servant, he set out on the road home.

How surprised this sinner must have felt when, while he was still traveling homeward, his father ran up and embraced him. While the son had been wasting his time and money in a foreign land, his father had been on the lookout. He'd foreseen what would happen and wanted to intervene in his son's hard life as soon as possible. All he'd looked for was repentance in the boy's heart.

Before the prodigal could spit out more than his admission of sin, his father sent servants to get a robe, shoes, and a ring symbolic of authority. He ordered a celebration feast, too.

Naturally, someone had to pour cold water on the festivities. The upright elder brother came back just in time to learn what had happened. When he found out that his brother was back, anger darkened his face. He sat outside and sulked. A servant must have let the father know about his elder son, for he came out to lovingly invite him to the celebration. Immediately, the son who up to then had done no wrong let his father know just how shortchanged he felt. He'd never had so much as a young goat for a feast with his friends, and here the sinner got the fatted calf cooked for dinner. Was that fair?

The father reminded the son that everything he had was

his—indeed, the good son had not spent his inheritance, and the younger son wouldn't have a bit of what was left. But how could this tender father fail to celebrate when his lost son returned?

The story ends there. We don't know if the younger son worked hard to build his own financial future, or if the elder brother forgave him. What we do know is that the father, who is a picture of God, loved both sons enough to forgive them completely.

When you read the story, are you the prodigal or the upright elder brother? Are you aware of your sin or of your own goodness? Whether you sin with ease and remorsefully turn back to God in repentance, or you tend to think too much of your own righteousness and hard-heartedly expect others to pay, forgiveness is yours. All you need do is turn to the Father in love. He forgives both wastrels and critics.

THE PUBLICAN

Two men went up into the temple to pray;
the one a Pharisee, and the other a publican.

LUKE 18:10 KJV

Contrast a first-century Pharisee and a publican (or tax
collector). One, an upstanding member of the community,
prays frequently and seeks to obey the law. The other works
for the Romans, who oppress his people, and rarely sets foot
in the Temple.

The highly religious Pharisee felt he had an edge on
those who engaged in obvious sins like adultery or extortion.
As he bragged to God of his own goodness, he denigrated
the tax collector, who obviously couldn't meet that holiness
standard.

The humble publican hardly raised his eyes as he
worshipped in the Temple. What was he doing there, laden
with all his sins? He understood his own lack of worth, and sin
bore him down so heavily that he barely whispered his need for
mercy into God's ear. The publican compared himself to God,
not another human, and he came up far short.

As Jesus told this parable and praised the humble
publican, He shocked His righteous audience. After all,
they were used to thinking highly of their own attempts
to please God, and wasn't obedience a good thing? But
no person lives sinlessly. Every believer humbly needs to
recognize the temptation to sin that sits constantly at the
heart's door.

THE RICH FOOL

*"But God said to him, 'Fool! This night your
soul will be required of you; then whose will
those things be which you have provided?' "*

LUKE 12:20 NKJV

Andrew Carnegie believed "the man who dies thus rich dies
disgraced." In Luke 12:13–21, it appears we have a man
who didn't quite subscribe to that philosophy.

Quite possibly, this fellow wasn't even miserly; he may
have been quite generous to others as God blessed him.
But he still became all too comfortable, all too self-satisfied,
all too self-absorbed. He may have hit a point in his life
when he no longer cared much about giving. He had all he
needed and then some. Why bother? He was preoccupied
with how he would store all his excess.

We're told that God had something to say to this man.
It began with, "Fool!" Having another person call you
a fool is one thing. Having God call you a fool is quite
another.

Why was God so harsh? For one thing, this man
was "goods-centered" instead of God-centered. It isn't
wicked to be rich, but it is wicked to be selfish. This
man never thought to ask the One responsible for all his
blessings what he should do with his wealth. He failed to
acknowledge that only God can fill the void within us. He
also failed to prepare for eternity. He clearly had only this
life in view.

Jesus warns us, "So is he who lays up treasure for himself, and is not rich toward God" (Luke 12:21 NKJV). Are we taking Him seriously?

THE RICH YOUNG MAN

So [Jesus] said to [the rich young man], "Why do you call Me good? No one is good but One, that is, God."

MATTHEW 19:17 NKJV

You're a young and wealthy man with a position of prestige. You've heard about this new Rabbi who is rapidly becoming known for His teaching and His healing. You want to meet Him, so you seek Him out. When you find Him, you pose what seems like an innocent question. Wanting to impress Him, you begin with, "Good Teacher." Number one mistake! You're surprised when Jesus says, "Why do you call Me good? No one is good but One, that is, God" (Matthew 19:17 NKJV). Little do you know that Jesus has just revealed to you the primary obstacle to faith in God. You're trusting in your own goodness to get you through heaven's gates.

"Oh," you say, "I've kept all the commandments since I was a tot." Have you? You must have been sleeping in synagogue the day Psalm 14:3 was read. It says, "There is no one who does good, not even one."

Full of yourself, you ask Jesus what more you could possibly do. "Sell everything you own and follow Me," He says. "Oh no," you say, "not that. I couldn't." Couldn't you? Do you walk away sad because you have great possessions; or do they have you?

SAMSON

And it came to pass, when [Delilah] pestered [Samson] daily with her words and pressed him, so that his soul was vexed to death, that he told her all his heart.

JUDGES 16:16–17 NKJV

He was a man of incomparable strength, dedicated to the Lord from birth as a Nazirite. Almost single-handedly, he valiantly waged war against the Philistines. No one could touch Samson or bring him down—no one, that is, except himself and his own weakness.

The angel of the Lord had appeared to Samson's barren mother and told her she would give birth to a son. He also gave her special prenatal instructions, because her son would be set apart for special service to the Lord.

Samson was born during a time in the history of Israel when "everyone did what was right in his own eyes" (Judges 17:6 NKJV). For forty years prior to Samson's birth, the children of Israel had sinned greatly against God. As a result, God allowed the dreaded Philistines to dominate them.

It wasn't long before Samson's feats of physical strength gained him a reputation among his own people and the

Philistines. He became a real thorn in the Philistines' side. As he wreaked havoc among them time and again, they became obsessed with doing away with this mighty Hebrew upstart. They went looking for flaws in Samson, and sure enough, they found some.

Sampson's physical strength made him and others vulnerable. Impressed with his own might, Samson became rather self-centered. Oftentimes this flaw was detrimental to those closest to him (see Judges 15). Worst of all was his bent toward sexual immorality. This flaw led to his downfall.

Samson liked women, and no doubt they liked him, too, given his reputation. Because unlawful intermingling had occurred between the Israelites and the Philistines, Samson had a much wider (and deadlier!) field to play. Sure enough, he set his sights on a Philistine beauty named Delilah. Evidently, she bewitched him. When Samson's Philistine foes found out about this affair, they hatched a plot. Money talks, and they paid Delilah well for her services. "Tell me the secret of your strength," she purred demurely. Ever thought about how superficial the web of a seductress is? Delilah, trained in the art of seductive nagging, spun her web skillfully. Finally, the mighty man from the tribe of Dan had had enough. He bared his most cherished secret, and the rest is history. His enemies enslaved him and blinded him—but he killed more Philistines in his death than in his life (Judges 16:30).

Samson fell for one of the subtlest and oldest traps ever. We have no strength but God's to keep our sexual drive from going into overdrive and entrapping us!

*So in the course of time Hannah conceived
and gave birth to a son. She named him Samuel,
saying, "Because I asked the LORD for him."*

1 SAMUEL 1:20

Samuel's name means "heard of God." But this prophet didn't just hear of God; he did God's will in a time of great civil unrest.

Samuel's mother knew that God had heard her request for a child, so she dedicated her child to Him. Because of this dedication, the boy grew up in the household of Eli the priest. Because Eli's own sons were unfaithful, God spoke to Samuel instead and made him a prophet.

Young Samuel saw the Philistines constantly battling his nation, and Israel was always on the losing end. So Samuel called Israel to renounce idol worship, and they did. For the first time in years, Israel won a battle over the attacking Philistines.

As God's prophet and judge, Samuel played a key role in building the nation of Israel. For many years, he ruled over the nation as their judge. But when he was old and his sons did not follow his good leadership example, the people asked Samuel to give them a king, as the other nations around them had. God warned that they'd have problems with kings, but He gave them Saul to rule over them, and Samuel anointed him.

Though King Saul started out well, before long he

became caught up in his own power and he turned from God. Though Samuel, his spiritual adviser, grieved the infidelity of the king, God had the prophet anoint David as king in Saul's place.

But David had to fight for his throne. Once again, strife destroyed the peace of Israel. Before David had consolidated his power, Saul died, and "all Israel. . .mourned for him" (1 Samuel 25:1 ESV). By the time of Samuel's death, the Israelites had again begun to worship idols.

Samuel is a fine example of a man who remained faithful, though he did not live in an ideal world. Although his own connection with God was clear, the people whose lives he directed were less than faithful. Though King Saul's rule seemed so promising, the leader designed to replace the elderly Samuel failed miserably.

But no matter who battled around him, Samuel remained true to the Lord. The prophet's message never changed. Neither did his devotion to the One who was primary in his life.

When we face times of strife and stress, do we blame God and immediately turn from Him, or like Samuel, do we trust that God will guide us through? Samuel may not have seen David take the throne, but because God is faithful, he knew it would happen.

SAUL, KING OF ISRAEL

He had a son named Saul, an impressive young
man without equal among the Israelites—
a head taller than any of the others.

1 SAMUEL 9:2

Saul is the Bible's promising politician gone bad. When
Saul came to Israel's throne, he didn't have a lot to
recommend him. Sure, he was good-looking and tall, and
his dad was wealthy, but what leadership experience did
he have? Yet all Israel, fed up with the corrupt rule of the
prophet Samuel's sons and constantly battling numerous
enemies, looked forward to having him in charge. Hope
filled the air in Israel when Saul went hunting down some
missing donkeys and ended up being anointed king by the
prophet Samuel.

At first, it was obvious that God's Spirit was on
the new king. Saul became an effective warrior for his
beleaguered nation. But as time went on, his subjects found
him less successful spiritually than militarily. Saul began
by defeating the Ammonites, but when the Philistines
attacked, Saul became impatient for battle and took it upon
himself to perform the sacrifice that Samuel had promised
to make. As neither priest nor prophet, Saul did not have
this right. So when Samuel came, he warned Saul that God
sought a man after His own heart to be king—and that
man was not Saul.

Meanwhile, Saul's son Jonathan began a foray that led

to the Philistines' defeat. But a foolish vow his father made almost cost Jonathan his life. Only the rebellion of the army, in Jonathan's defense, brought Saul to his senses.

Warfare continued as Saul defeated more of Israel's enemies. God commanded the king to attack the Amalekites and destroy all the people and their livestock. But Saul disobeyed, keeping their king alive, along with the best of the Amalekites' cattle. Samuel confronted the king with his disobedience. After a halfhearted admission of guilt, Saul saw his partial obedience as a good thing and could not understand the prophet's concern. Then this brave warrior-king became a coward as he blamed his own actions on the people.

Saul had rejected God, Samuel announced, so God had rejected him as king. If Saul thought he'd had opposition from Israel's enemies, he was about to face a new, internal conflict that would be even worse. For God sent Samuel to anoint the shepherd David as king in Saul's place.

Deserted by God's Spirit, Saul became prone to depression. To ease his suffering, Saul's attendants suggested they hire a harpist to soothe the king's disease. And whom did they choose but David, the man God had anointed king in Saul's place. David not only sang to the king; he became the people's favorite war commander. When his subjects praised David's deeds, Saul became jealous, and as his madness increased, he attempted to take the life of the shepherd turned warrior. Then, to trap David, Saul gave him his daughter Michal as his wife—a relationship that turned out badly for everyone involved.

Saul's son Jonathan favored David, creating tense moments within the royal family. Finally, Jonathan helped his friend escape. From then on, Saul and David's disagreements took place on the battlefield. But even when Saul could have been at his mercy, David spared God's anointed.

As the Philistines again gathered against Israel, Saul sought a word from God on the battle's outcome. When no response came, the king looked to the witch of Endor for an answer. She called up a spirit that Saul believed was Samuel, but the king probably would have preferred not to hear his news: Saul would lose the battle.

That prediction came true. In defeat, Saul took his own life, and the Philistines made a grisly show of his body—and those of his sons killed in battle—on the walls of the city of Beth Shan.

Though Saul's son Ish-bosheth ruled briefly in Israel, eventually David became king of both Judah and Israel.

Saul reminds us that starting well is not enough. Lifelong consistency of belief is what God calls us to. Every day, we need to serve Him well.

SILAS

*About midnight Paul and Silas were praying and
singing hymns. . . . Suddenly there was such a violent
earthquake that. . .all the prison doors flew open.*

ACTS 16:25–26

The apostle Paul's companion after the split with Barnabas,
Silas crossed much of the Mediterranean world with him.
Their mission began when Paul and Barnabas came to
Jerusalem to discuss what the church expected of the
Gentiles, and the Jerusalem council decided that Silas
should return to Antioch with them.

Shortly afterward, Paul set out with Silas for a tour
through Syria and Cilicia. Later, Paul received a call to
Macedonia, and Silas was one of the band of men who
accompanied him.

In Philippi, they met an irritating slave girl with a
demonic spirit that predicted the future. Paul cleansed her
of that possession, and as a result, he and Silas were beaten
and tossed into the jail, then put in the stocks. Together
they praised God and remained in prison to preach to the
jailer.

Silas went to a lot of trouble to serve God, crossing land
and sea with Paul, and got little public commendation. Do
we need attention to feel we're important Christians, or will
we be faithful like Silas?

SIMEON

[Simeon] took Him up in his arms and blessed God and said:
"Lord, now You are letting Your servant depart in peace,
according to Your word; for my eyes have seen Your salvation."

LUKE 2:28–30 NKJV

Throughout the ages, the children of Israel anticipated the coming of One called the Messiah. The Old Testament is full of references to Him; the prophets spoke at length about Him. The Virgin Mary had the singular privilege of bearing Him.

A heavenly messenger informed a man named Simeon that he would not see death until he saw the Messiah. We're not told very much about this aged man. Scripture says that he was righteous and devout and looking forward to the Messiah's arrival. Then came the day when, led by the Holy Spirit, Simeon entered the Temple in Jerusalem to find a couple with a baby. It was the moment of moments for Simeon. Here was the Messiah at last!

Imagine a joy that makes you perfectly resigned to depart this life. That's what Simeon felt as he took the baby reverently up in his arms. God led Simeon to recognize the Messiah and to proclaim words about this child that astonished all who heard, but most of all his parents. "This Child is destined for the fall and rising of many in Israel, and for a sign which will be spoken against," prophesied Simeon (Luke 2:34 NKJV).

Time has borne out Simeon's prophecy. Who do you say this child was?

SIMON OF CYRENE

They found a man of Cyrene, Simon by name.
Him they compelled to bear His cross.

MATTHEW 27:32 NKJV

We have more questions than answers about this man Simon, who appears briefly in Jesus' life, at a moment of pain, as the Lord was forced to carry the cross to Golgotha.

Simon, who had two sons, Alexander and Rufus, hailed from a large city in what would be modern-day Libya. Many Jews had settled in Cyrene, so perhaps he'd traveled with a group to Jerusalem for the Passover. But here he stands alone. Once we've looked at these bare facts, reported in a single verse in each synoptic Gospel, we have scripture's whole record.

Simon was simply an innocent bystander, dragged into the Crucifixion story by Roman soldiers who plucked him out of a crowd and made him carry the thirty- to forty-pound cross. The duty they called him to was thoroughly unpleasant and unexpected.

Was Simon a Christian? We don't know. But he reminds us that no matter what happens to us, God is still in control. Before time began, God designed His plan of salvation; and though Simon's part was a surprise to him, it wasn't a surprise to God.

If God pulled us out of a crowd to do His will, would we be ready to feel the cross's splinters in our hands?

SOLOMON

Then David comforted Bathsheba his wife, and went in to her and lay with her. So she bore a son, and he called his name Solomon. Now the LORD loved him.

2 SAMUEL 12:24 NKJV

"Give me the whole world but not God, and I'll still be miserable," warns Solomon's worldly and sophisticated but empty life.

But it wasn't always that way. From the day of Solomon's birth, God loved him. Despite the sexual sin his parents had fallen into, God had forgiven and blessed David and Bathsheba with this son. And David and his wife weren't the only ones: "The LORD loved him" is a wonderful testimony to the start of a great relationship between God and Prince Solomon.

Just before David died, many of his sons tried to grab the throne. But the king fulfilled an old promise he'd made to Bathsheba and had Solomon crowned as his heir. As a last gift, David provided detailed guidelines that would help his son rule well. Feeling honored, the new king started out, in the flush of youth, with many good intentions.

Shortly after Solomon's ascension to the throne, God asked him what he wanted. Given carte blanche, the king requested wisdom with which to rule the people. Pleased by this unselfish choice, God promised Solomon wisdom—and much more. Empowered by the Spirit, Solomon made wise choices for his people and penned the books of Proverbs, Song of Solomon, and Ecclesiastes. And the Lord added prosperity to the king's many other blessings.

Solomon's glorious reign expanded Israel's power and instituted beautiful building projects. After he made an alliance with Pharaoh and married his daughter, Solomon built both a new temple and a palace. An alliance with Hiram, king of Tyre, gave Solomon access to wonderful building materials and the craftsmen to make use of them. Within seven years, the first Temple was completed, and the workmen began a thirteen-year palace-building project.

At the highest point in his career, Solomon dedicated the new Temple. He began with a wonderful worship service and called the people to believe steadfastly in their Lord. A huge, impressive sacrifice followed, and celebration broke out among the Israelites. God promised that the obedience of Solomon and his heirs would establish his throne forever. But if they turned from God, Israel would be cut off from the land, and God would reject the Temple.

Solomon's fame and fortune spread. The Queen of Sheba conferred with him, and his riches surpassed those of every other ruler. But to make alliances that expanded his power, Solomon married seven hundred wives and took three hundred concubines, actions that flew in the face of God's commands concerning marriage.

For years, Solomon remained faithful. At first, he seemed untouched by his wives' various religions, but as time passed, he began building altars to their gods so they could worship their pagan deities. Then he began to feel the attraction of these gods himself and worshipped them. The results of his unfaithfulness appear in Ecclesiastes, which pictures a cynical, doubtful ruler who has seen the world and discovered its emptiness.

This partial commitment angered God. So He raised up enemies against Israel, and Solomon's nation was attacked from within and without. After forty years of rule, Solomon died, and his son Rehoboam assumed his embattled throne.

Solomon grew up in a believing household, and God blessed him, but when the wealthy, successful king failed to flee from sin, a promising spiritual relationship slipped into compromise.

Can we relate to Solomon's story? We, too, have been given much, but it's still easy to find ourselves making something other than God central to our lives. Though we've served Him for many years, we can never relax our vigilance. Satan stands at the door, ready to slide back in and attack.

When we're young and enthusiastic, it's easy to think that our spiritual success is a piece of cake. But faith in God requires that we look toward the long haul. When life is difficult and a spiritual desert faces us, will we be as strong? Only God's Spirit gives us the determination and dedication we need.

STEPHEN

Now Stephen, a man full of God's grace and power,
did great wonders and miraculous signs among the people.

ACTS 6:8

Stephen, blessed by God, had a powerful message. But not everyone liked his words. The Synagogue of the Freedmen objected to his Christian testimony, not because they thought it didn't make sense, but because they could not refute it.

So, like many faithful believers, Stephen found himself in hot water with his opponents, who dragged him before the Sanhedrin. The synagogue attendees found a few immoral men willing to accuse Stephen of blasphemy against God and the Law. When questioned, Stephen presented the Jewish rulers with a wonderful testimony based on the Law of God. But that didn't make them any happier, for he accused them of resisting God. Finally, Stephen saw a vision of Jesus and proclaimed that He stood at God's right hand.

At this, his enemies covered their ears and dragged him out to stone him. The dying Stephen asked for forgiveness for his attackers.

Stephen's testimony is a shining example of faith. Don't we all wish we'd respond as powerfully in the face of persecution? The Holy Spirit empowered Stephen, and He strengthens us, too. But we cannot wait until persecution arises to seek God. Daily we need to draw near Him and seek His filling. Then, when a moment of attack comes, we will be ready.

THOMAS

And Thomas answered and said unto him,
My Lord and my God.

JOHN 20:28 KJV

Thomas was a man who liked to see things plainly
and clearly. When anything began to look muddy, he
confronted it directly. But his attitudes haven't made him
an admired Bible character, because we prefer to read about
people who trust and never question: "God said it; I believe
it; that settles it."

Thomas was a believer. When Jesus was headed into
danger, going back to Bethany to raise Lazarus, Thomas
willingly accompanied his Master to an expected death. It
was a plain thing he could understand and face bravely. But
when Jesus began talking vaguely about going to prepare
a place for His disciples, Thomas wanted more facts: How
would they know the way to Jesus? No pie-in-the-sky
religion for this disciple.

Thomas is best known for not being with the other
disciples when Jesus made a post-Resurrection appearance.
Again Thomas doubted what he could not see, until Jesus
stood before him. Then "doubting Thomas" immediately
went to the other extreme, accepting Jesus as the living Lord.

Like Thomas, we often prefer hard facts to hard faith.
But, like him, are we willing to accept Jesus' statement that
those who do not see are blessed? Are we ready to become
one of the unseeing believers?

TIMOTHY

For this reason I am sending to you Timothy, my son whom I love, who is faithful in the Lord. He will remind you of my way of life in Christ Jesus, which agrees with what I teach everywhere in every church.

1 CORINTHIANS 4:17

As a young man, Timothy received high praise from the exacting apostle Paul. So close did he and the apostle become that the peripatetic Paul thought of Timothy as a son, brought him on numerous journeys with him, and sent him as an envoy, too.

Young Timothy didn't come from the "perfect Christian home." His Jewish mother, Eunice, became a Christian, but the little we know of his father suggests he was an unbelieving Greek. However, his grandmother Lois also believed, so spiritually, Timothy had at least two family members in his corner.

Timothy joined Paul on his second and third missionary journeys and part of the fourth. When they were not together, Paul wrote the two biblical books that bear the young pastor's name. The advice he offered has encouraged many church leaders.

Though Timothy seemed to be somewhat timid, in God's hand he became an example to all leaders. Despite our limitations and failures, are we willing to let God shape our lives as He will?

Paul. . .to Titus, my true child in a common faith.
TITUS 1:1, 4 ESV

Along with Timothy, Titus, a Greek, joined Paul on the second and third missionary journeys and part of the fourth. Despite church contentions about Gentiles, Paul supported Titus and refused to make him be circumcised.

Paul must have trusted Titus deeply, for he sent him on special missions that would have taken tact and an ability to relate to people. First, he sent Titus to the Corinthians, bearing a very sensitive letter. Paul had the unhappy task of correcting the Corinthians, who had fallen into sin. So he needed a man who would treat them both firmly and tenderly. The mission went well, the Corinthians repented, and after reporting back to Paul, Titus returned to Corinth with another minister, possibly Luke, to encourage the church.

Finally, Paul sent Titus to Crete to appoint elders in the church. While Titus was there, Paul penned the letter that bears Titus's name, a brief epistle that pictures what a church should look like.

Could we be trusted with a delicate mission for God? Let's study to be sensitive to others, considerate of their needs, and concerned for their spiritual walk. Then, like Titus, we may be used by God in just such a situation.

URIAH

David sent someone to find out about her.
The man said, "Isn't this Bathsheba, the daughter
of Eliam and the wife of Uriah the Hittite?"

2 SAMUEL 11:3

Uriah the Hittite was not an Israelite, yet he proved more upright than the Jewish king he served. This foreigner was part of David's royal guard, carefully picked men who were much more than common soldiers (see 2 Samuel 23:18–39). But while Uriah was on a military campaign, King David glimpsed Uriah's lovely wife, Bathsheba, as she bathed on her roof, and he lusted for her. He brought her to his palace, slept with her, and returned her home. Then she discovered she was pregnant.

David wanted to make it appear that the child was Uriah's, but though his dedicated soldier returned to Jerusalem at David's command, he would not give in to the comforts of home when his comrades were on the battlefront. So David placed Uriah in the heat of battle, and he was killed. After he died, the king married Bathsheba.

Uriah, a foreigner who served the Lord by protecting the king, had a focus on fidelity that escaped his master. The most unlikely person may serve God faithfully, while a much-honored one fails. Remember, God is no respecter of persons, and even the humblest may do His will.

Do we recognize the importance of humble belief over social standing? Are we looking to the things of God's kingdom or to earthly importance?

THE WIDOW OF NAIN'S SON

And when He came near the gate of the city, behold, a dead man was being carried out, the only son of his mother; and she was a widow. And a large crowd from the city was with her.

LUKE 7:12 NKJV

As her son was carried out of the city gate, the widow stared destitution in the face. She had no career opportunities to speak of, and she was an older woman. She had plenty of support on the day of her son's burial, but who would care for her from then on?

Jesus saw the situation and had compassion. "Do not weep," he told the grieving mother. He touched the young man's coffin and told him to rise. Immediately, the boy sat up and began to speak. Jesus reunited mother and son as the crowd glorified God and praised Jesus as a prophet.

If the crowds were amazed, how much more the son must have felt. Reunited with his needy mother, he must have wondered why Jesus had chosen him for resurrection, of all the people who had died that day.

We, too, have been raised to new life. "Why did Jesus choose me instead of another?" we may ask ourselves. Like the widow's son, we can only make the most of the days that God has given us. God's choice is always wise.

ZACCHAEUS

Now behold, there was a man named Zacchaeus
who was a chief tax collector, and he was rich.

LUKE 19:2 NKJV

"Zacchaeus was a wee little man, a wee little man was he,"
many of us sang as children. As we grew, this wee man
stayed in our hearts, the sign of a disadvantaged fellow who
had plenty of money. For not only was Zacchaeus small; he
also had a small life, ostracized by other Jews, who resented
his work for the occupying Romans. Who among us cannot
relate to this underdog who won't be kept down?

When Jesus came to town, the little man determined
to see Him and climbed a tree (maybe that's why we liked
him so much when we were children). Jesus saw Zacchaeus,
called to him, and invited Himself to his home. No host
could have been happier. Zacchaeus quickly repented and
promised to make restitution for more than the amount of
money of which he'd defrauded people. Salvation came to
the unpopular tax collector—suddenly he was friends with
Jesus.

We, too, began as Zacchaeus did, separated from God
and out of touch with humanity. Called by Jesus, we leaped
to believe and, perhaps more slowly than the tax collector,
changed our lives. We became friends with Jesus, and joy
filled our lives. Are we living in that joy today?

ZACHARIAS, FATHER OF JOHN THE BAPTIST

And Zacharias said to the angel, "How shall I know this?
For I am an old man, and my wife is well advanced in years."

LUKE 1:18 NKJV

"Is anything too hard for the LORD?" asks God in Genesis
18:14. These words were spoken by God to Abram's wife,
Sarai, who laughed at the thought of having a baby in her
old age.

Centuries later, Zacharias and his wife, Elizabeth,
were on in years. Elizabeth was barren and already beyond
the point of having children. You can imagine, then,
how surprised Zacharias was when told by the archangel
Gabriel that Elizabeth would bear them a son. Wouldn't
the supernatural appearance of an angel be enough to
underscore the certainty of what Zacharias had been told?
But no, Zacharias wanted proof. Gabriel gave him more
than proof. He made him unable to speak. Not until his
son, John, was born would he regain his ability to speak,
and then he had nothing to say but glory to God!

Is anything too hard for the Lord? Zacharias would
answer with an emphatic "No!" He had witnessed the
undeniable power of God—a God who keeps His word.
Do we need an angel to appear in order for us to take
God's word seriously?

ZECHARIAH THE PROPHET

In the eighth month of the second year of Darius,
the word of the LORD came to Zechariah the son of Berechiah,
the son of Iddo the prophet, saying, "The LORD
has been very angry with your fathers."

ZECHARIAH 1:1–2 NKJV

It was business as usual in Israel: The people were following the bad example of their forefathers. But neither the prophet Zechariah nor the Lord wanted it to stay that way.

That's why God again spoke to His people. He not only told them that their fathers were wrong, He also called them to repent.

A postexilic prophet-priest and a contemporary of Haggai and Zerubbabel, Zechariah held out hope to the people of Jerusalem during the later part of the era of the rebuilding of the Temple. For some years, progress on the building project had faltered. Then it stopped altogether. Now the people needed encouragement to build again.

Zechariah's message looks forward to the future and includes numerous messianic references. The prophet looks toward the work God will do in his own generation and beyond that to the coming salvation of God.

Like the people of Zechariah's age, we, too, falter and face terrible trials. Are we fainting? God did not desert Zechariah's people, and He will not forget us either. Look to the future with hope!

Also from
Barbour Publishing

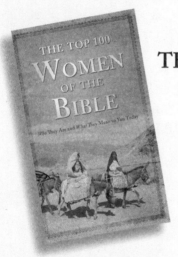

THE TOP 100
WOMEN
OF THE
BIBLE

ISBN 978-1-61626-249-5